DECIPHERING PETROGLYPHS

Ancient Universal Language of Man

Chris Hegg

Rowe Publishing

Copyright © 2015 by Christopher Hegg.
All rights reserved.

SOFTCOVER
ISBN 13: 978-1-939054-45-6
ISBN 10: 1-939054-45-1

HARDCOVER
ISBN 13: 978-1-939054-53-1
ISBN 10: 1-939054-53-2

No portion of this work may be used or reproduced in any manner whatsoever without written permission, except in the case of brief quotations embodied in articles and reviews from the Publisher.

Visit the author's website for more information about his ongoing research, follow him on social media, sign up for his blog, and contact information for speaking arrangements.

www.authorchrishegg.com

1 3 5 7 9 8 6 4 2

Printed in the United States of America
Published by

www.rowepub.com
Stockton, Kansas

Dedication

For Tyler,
Dawson, Pepper,
and Dede,
you are my everything!

Contents

Preface. 1
    2   *Babel*
    4   *Ancients*

Introduction 9
   11 *Background*
   11 *Basic Code*
   13 *First Breakthrough*

Universal Language Symbols. 15
   15 *Sign*
   16 *Modern Images*
   18 *Visual Stimuli*

Arrowheads. 19
Body Dexterity. 22
Core Starter Symbols 27
Hand Movement. 30
Symbol Categories. 34
   34 *Core Symbol Paths and Points*
   35 *Multiple Symbols*
   35 *Complex Symbols*
   36 *Combined Symbols*

Symbol Use Similarity Requirements. 37
   37 *Natural Environment*
   38 *Rock Incorporation*

Story Setup 39
Rock Layout. 42
   43 *Scratches*
   44 *Types of Media Dictate Types of Symbol Creation*

Symbol Meanings 46
Rain into Ice 51
Circles 53
    54   *First Petroglyph Site*
Fire 56
Understanding a Small Petroglyph Is Important 58
    60   *Paths As Trails*
Curves Into Quadrupeds 61
    64   *Quadruped Section Meanings*
    65   *Travel by Ship Quadrupeds*
    66   *Travel by Land Quadrupeds*
    70   *A Group in Trouble*
    71   *Pack Animals*
Movements of Celestial Bodies 72
Other Movements Represented 73
    74   *Easy reading*
The Moon 75
    79   *Software Help*
Moon Count 80
    83   *Vandalism Results*
Stars 84
    85   *Archeoastronomy*
    87   *Star Date*
The Polar Stars 90
Seasons 94
    95   *Core Combinations*
    95   *Winter*
    95   *Spring*
    96   *Summer*
    96   *Autumn*
    97   *Nature Tied Symbols*
3D Newer Style of the Same Symbols 98
Seasonal Day Counters 100
Circumference Data 102
    104   *Contracting and Expanding Paths*
    104   *Circumference Radiating Shadow Lines*
Cassiopeia Included as the Other Time Keeper 106
Rock Shadow Incorporation 109
    110   *Shadow Lines*
Bracketing with Season Symbols 112

Combining Different Season Symbols Into One 114
    114   *Other Season Reference*
    116   *Daily Tracking Symbols*
    117   *Daily Tracking Symbols*
    120   *Vertical Shadow Paths*
    121   *Symbol Design Modified for Natural Shadow Shapes*
    122   *Multiple Site Time Segmentation*
Squares of Land 124
Gravesite Squares 127
Squares for Sun Tracking 129
Month Symbols 131
    131   *Continuous Paths*
    132   *Spirals*
    133   *Analemma Into Spirals*
    135   *Shadows*
    135   *Direction of Spiral*
    138   *Crossover*
    142   *Equality of Season Month*
    143   *Circumference Data of Months*
2D and 3D Representation of the Symbols 144
Megalithic Usage 146
Micro Decipherment Secrets 148
Tattooing Practice 152
Graveyard Symbols 153
    153   *Flowers*
    155   *Holy Site Warning Symbol*
    156   *The Dead Honored*
    157   *Central Graveyards*
    158   *Graveyard Types*
Younger Petroglyphs 161
    161   *Spanish Miners*
    162   *Defensive*
    163   *Wagons*
    164   *Mammoths*
Hands 166
    167   *Blocking*
    167   *Solar Eclipses*
The Foot 172
Petroglyph Location 175
    176   *Floating Cities*
    177   *World Trade*

Trade Routes 178
     181   *Death Valley Giants Account*
     183   *Lakes of Ancient Times*
Site Location 187
Lake Petroglyphs 190
Modern Thoughts 194
     194   *Pointer*
Hidden Caves 200
     200   *Lizards*
Themes 205
     206   *Snake and Tarantula Harvesting and War*
     210   *Earthquake Camp*
     213   *Rose Bush Site*
     219   *Crop Growing*
     220   *Trading Vessel Demise*
     220   *Graveyards*
     221   *Deer refuge*
     221   *Ancient Great Lakes Fishing*
     222   *Defensive Strongholds*
     223   *Fish Harvesting*
     225   *Fremont's Cannon*
     230   *Spanish*
     231   *Alien Visitors*
     233   *The Ancient Floating City of the Pyramid*
     234   *Trains*
     236   *Lake Fowl Hunting*
     237   *Obsidian Mining*
Acknowledgments 239
Index 240

Preface

My purpose in writing this book is to teach the original Universal Language of man! It is made to lay down in writing the reasoning behind the symbols so dismissed by academia in the past as drug induced and shamanism drawings. Magic, spirit visions, early artistic attempts are all simple ideals to staple onto every unknown writing system not understood. Yet someone once spent much labor and time on these archives carved in stone to assure it would be remembered down through the ages. It is clear that once anyone spent enough time roaming and visiting these sites, the similarities that exist would see repeatability that is absolutely unavoidable. He or she would quickly realize unscripted squiggly lines are not what petroglyphs represent. Seeing a circle or line sequence again and again in the same area of the rock, in sites located thousands of miles apart, is not coincidence. Sooner or later you begin to question why scholars continue to write that one drugged shaman draws just like the other drug-addicted shaman a half a globe away. Read the book *A Guide to Rock Art Sites* by David S. Whitley to really internalize sacred rituals, shamanism, and vision quest petroglyph labeling. How could humans who are experiencing drug-induced hallucinations precisely and laboriously draw intricate and repeatable symbol creations again and again? Have you, in a sober mind, tried to work on something that was intricate and laborious? Carving rock is difficult. The miniature reproduction petroglyphs that I build are as close to the real thing as possible at approximately 1:20th the scale. I have never wanted to attempt a full scale panel due to this great effort. It is one thing to write about something without living it and doing it, because you think you are right. It is another to go try it before you write it.

We will begin our journey of the observation of petroglyph symbols not at the birth of Christ or the building of the pyramids at Giza; Stonehenge in

England or of New Grange in Ireland. We will go much further back! Beyond the collections of written knowledge to a time of man now long lost to the world. A world beyond 16,000 years ago to the time of the last Ice Age when man survived a brutal landscape in the harshest of regions and flourished as the first empires!

Out of the darkness of the last Ice Age we came into our own light, but now sit pondering the great ancient sites of the world asking questions: Who built them and what do they signify?

Babel

I will attempt to show what existed before this *information darkness*. A time when Universal Language was made and taught to all the people of every land, so such things as global trading and peace could be accomplished. This was not an esoteric code, it was meant to be globally learned. The Hebrew Bible describes this Universal Language existing in Babel as they tried to make a "tower" to the heavens and the language was ultimately changed to many different languages. The separate groups were divided for this effort and spread to the corners of the globe to be forever lost. The language was used before this by cultures to build magnificent monoliths for understanding the universal movement of time on every continent in a global setting not seen since, well, after Babel, (the legendary homeland where the tower to Heaven was being built and stopped by God: Gen. 11:4–9). I believe that the ancient history of all these monumental undertakings everywhere, to "reach" to the heavens, survived as the story in the Bible.

This combined effort to make a global capacity of understanding of the heavens that would last eternity, was thwarted sometime between then and now. The result is the loss of the old world's efforts and above all the loss of our global connection of peace, by means of the Universal Language, which in turn allowed trade and expanding ideas from the global community. Peace was evident by the literally thousands of mega-projects developed by independent societies from every corner of the globe but incorporating shared ideas. The simple fact that every one of those projects when compared with the Universal Language identify as the SAME language symbols. Simply built of earthly materials in epic sized format compared to carved into rock to stand as much the test of time, as to weather some unknown calamity that would otherwise, and did, decimate all other manmade creations of that time! The information contained in the physical appearances and designs of these structures ARE the reproduced physical recreation of the Universal Language. These structures mimicking exactly the language is a fantastic combination relevant to their true purpose. This undertaking by all of the world has stood as the largest combined effort of man to accomplish something obviously

Photo 1

Photo 2

Photo 1 and 2 - Two petroglyph styles from the north and south parts of Nevada. Photo 1 image has obvious bodies drawn in full width whereas Photo 2 petroglyph uses only single lines, a concept I will discuss later.

magnificent and important. This also means it would have been one of the most conglomerated showing of peace man has ever seen. Our thinking today is slowly being purged of systemic higher educational instituted teaching that modern man could be the only ones to walk the earth "evolved" enough to even have the concept of simple art, family, death, and invention. The fact is ancient man was absolutely as smart or smarter in existing and conquering nature as we are. All new exploration into the past yields ever so slightly to the reality of it. I am stating here, one can live in the environment with information contained in the petroglyph LANGUAGE while firmly stating that little to nothing is useful to me in the information contained in most archaeological papers published on petroglyphs. There is probably more truth in fact that the educated works of many archeological papers were written by more drug induced trances than were any historic petroglyph panels!

Ancients

The ancients taught the Universal Language. There are sites dedicated as classrooms, but I suspect most childhood teaching was on panels with chalk and charcoal and dirt drawings as they went, and is now lost to us. Some history pelts of writing by ideogram do exist with family and tribe trekking around the globe and in North America.

Who were these distant people? I can only answer as the "ancients"—a group of races, like today, that managed their own territories. From mummified remains it is known there were dark-headed Caucasians and giants with red hair in the west. Legends of Indians have small people, white people of regular size, and giants living just thousands of years ago. Even Meriwether Lewis wrote of almost white, round-eyed tribes on his expedition. Such writings against this new land we call America may have been his demise. The designations by man of all of these lands around the globe make it absolute that territories had to be split up to keep proper control to the regions. Thus empires were born and even spurs of empires spread, because it happened in all of modern history when an empire grows too large. Although wars broke out, it is clear that monuments built by societies who had the means to do so, were constructed to survive the decimation of man and land thus proving mankind was united in an unprecedented effort to pass to us this knowledge.

When I ponder *why*, I am awestruck with the amazing efforts it took. *Why* is this information needed for us in the future? *Why* did they realize we needed to know this information? If this was the case, it was convincible to all on the globe that it was (1) needed, (2) was in fact going to happen, and possibly (3) it must be done by all in such a remarkable way so that such sites could not be walked away from with a shrug thousands of years later (which humans have an innate ability to ignore what they think is unimportant, because they can't understand it, like petroglyphs). They, the builders, would have been convinced their efforts would make a difference and be remembered through time and that, more importantly, would be understood in time to do something about it before it was too late. I am speculating that these are the reasons for all of the megaliths around the world that are similar and repeat the same information—a Universal Language. It is difficult to confirm events that without a doubt are going to come around again. And harder yet to determine such events that need the types of monuments seen in a global scale built thousands of years prior. Could their message be that a rogue planet's rotation, like the fabled Planet X, be coming back around again? Could the reality of severe global warming be cyclic and have catastrophic consequences to the world, so bad a future warning was needed to help us prepare? A return through a region of space, every so many thousands of years, consuming the globe into darkness, like some stories of old claim? A cyclic flipping of the Earth's magnetic poles causing global issues? Solar flares? Simple regional events spurring such builds just don't iron out enough to convince me that such an event would induce an entire population of man into caring enough to labor for a future world warning that such calamity happened to them and will happen to us?

I have a theory as to why the great Universal Language vanished by looking at the Bible's stories and today's evidence of these locations and people. The Bible tells of the uselessness and ego of man to build a massive stairway to Heaven in the Tower of Babel (Old Testament, Genesis I). It appears that every culture made monoliths and cities and dedicated much to build and leave behind the great showings of their cultures individuality and abilities—the Greeks, Romans, Polynesians, Aztecs, Mayans, Sumerians, and Egyptians all shown brilliance. Their knowledge of the cycles of life and the language made each try and show upon the world their cultures were as great as the next by doing these vast creations of stone. This over-usage of manpower and the land's resources led to ignoring other basic needs and harmony with the Earth. On Easter Island, for instance, they used up the resources constructing the megalith statues surrounding the island and to this day almost no trees exist. The tribe living there was nearly extinct by the time modern man found them. It should be noted that other Moai have been found on other islands, debunking the modern thought that Easter Island was secluded from travelling the rest of the ocean. The Inca's appear to have destroyed their entire jungle environment by making oven-baked brick for construction of their cities and temples that lead to the rebellion and abandonment of their empire ways. In every aspect, slowly killing themselves off to achieve these monuments. The resources committed to the build deforested whole regions and devastated food resources, eventually coming full circle to destroy the very empire everyone backed to build such accomplishments. Among many, the Polynesians, Myans, Aztec, and Egyptian lands were decimated, thought from erosion and other unbalanced effects of nature, from resource depletion due to monument building. These building projects were then considered very bad and man was punished for his commitment to such feats and the legends survived the times. Man mostly buried or destroyed these amazing accomplishments or simply walked away. In most instances the empire vanished as people walked away from it or destroyed it. As happened then it will happen again as man is predictable in the unyielding ways of group social behavior. Where culture becomes fixed, men in power become unyielding and there is no way out as a nation but to go along with it until the end is met and the group is no longer able to maintain those fixed ways. Ancient societies killed for sacrifice, were conquered by technologically superior neighbors, or died under geologic calamities such as Pompeii. Modern societies are economically and religiously tied as every world war and conflict depicts so clearly. As it is today, it was also in the past—economics of trade and religious differences spurred similar unrecorded wars.

It was the loss of the ice, and thus massive water runoff, from the last ice age, that erased much of the old knowledge of the Universal Language and the monuments and to why this was all done. As the ice and waters receded so did the super highways that connected us all. Where man once floated to each other in ease, the lakes and byways dried up and man had to walk. These distances of dry land finally ended such connections and the great rebirth of man began as the old knowledge slowly died away.

The Walker Lake Paiute Tribe met with "The Great Pathfinder" John C. Fremont, (a famous American military officer, politician, and western explorer who in 1845 made an expedition to map western territory sanctioned by the federal government) described in his book, *Memoirs of my life and times: John Charles Fremont* describing that the Paiute tribes gathered over 300 warriors from all over the Nevada western area to end the giants (Si-Te-Cah) once and for all due to their constant harassment of the Utes and rumored to even eat them. They caught 13 of the giants near the lake and drove the giant red heads back to the cave over 100 miles away where they burned brush in the opening to kill them after they would not surrender. They called them the Si-Te-Cah, which meant Tule eaters (an extinct type of stalk resembling a cat tail) because they ate tule and actually were said to LIVE on tule raft cities ON Pyramid Lake. The red hair of one was woven into the Chief's Princess dress (En.wikipedia.org/wiki/si-te-cah). The Paiutes, like most I've read about, told Fremont they did not write the petroglyphs and that they existed before they arrived 1,500 years prior and that they suspected the giants wrote them. They told of capturing one giant. They tortured him to death trying to find out what the petroglyphs meant, but the giant died not telling anything. They believed that if the petroglyphs could ever be read, it would bring peace on earth. These Utes told that all the tribes once talked the same language and that they could go by water to each other and visit easily. Then the waters dried up and it was too hard to walk to one another and so the tribes split, their languages changed, and war replaced brotherhood.

This reasoning is in most cultures verbal stories passed down since the beginning. Science is now quickly catching up with this and the dogma of stating a man walked in America 14,000-20,000 years ago in mass is "possible," but someday it will be old news. *Journal of Archaeological Science, Dating*

Abstract

On the west side of the Winnemucca Lake subbasin, Nevada, distinctive deeply carved meter-scale petroglyphs are closely spaced, forming panels on boulder-sized surfaces of a partially collapsed tufa mound. The large, complex motifs at this side are formed by deeply carved lines and cupules. A carbonate crust deposited between 10,200 and 9,800 calibrated years B.P. (ka) coats petroglyphs at the base of the mound between elevations of 1202 and 1206 m. Petroglyphs above the carbonate crust are carved into a branching form of carbonate that dates to 14.8 ka. Radiocarbon dates on a multiple-layered algal tufa on the east side of the basin, which formed at an elevation of 1205 m, as well as a sediment-core-based total inorganic carbon record for the period 17.0–9.5 ka indicate that water level in the Winnemucca Lake subbasin was constrained by spill over the Emerson Pass Sill (1207 m) for most of the time between 12.9 ± 0.3 and ≥9.2 ka. These and other data indicate that the lake in the Winnemucca Lake subbasin fell beneath its spill point between 14.8 and 13.2 ka and also between 11.3 and 10.5 ka (or between 11.5 and 11.1 ka), exposing the base of the collapsed tufa mound to petroglyph carving. The tufa-based 14C record supports decreased lake levels between 14.8–13.2 ka and 11.3–10.5 ka. Native American artifacts found in the Lahontan Basin date to the latter time interval. This does not rule out the possibility that petroglyph carving occurred between 14.8 and 13.2 ka when Pyramid Lake was relatively shallow and Winnemucca Lake had desiccated.

Source: *Journal of Archaeological Science, Dating North Americas Oldest Petroglyphs*

North Americas Oldest Petroglyphs, Winnemucca Lake Subbasin, Nevada, (Volume 40, Issue 12, Pages 4466-4476), shows new research of a petroglyph made BEFORE it was submerged by waters until 9,000+ years ago. The research of the tufa growth on the carvings show buildup growth developing after submersion at least 14,800 years ago.

Introduction

My strengths of decipherment began around 13 years of age. Years after I saw my first petroglyph shown to my Grandparents and I by an old Paiute Indian woman. I recall a very dusty and miserably hot sunny day when we drove out in an old faded yellow Apache pickup my Grandpa bought from the Forest Service. The truck had no air conditioning and as a kid I bacame carsick quite easily, but refused to ever be left behind. The dirt road seemingly went on forever as it led into the deepest of the valleys where no human lived within 25 miles. I remember how amazed I was at the size of the world and I was old enough to start remembering locations, and this was the furthest I remembered traveling to. The old woman was scary to me, talking light, but with a raspy voice and a smile that had few teeth. Being Paiute, she was heavy set and short with long hair down her face and she told us that she had a "snake stick." I knew then that she must be a witch and could turn that stick into a snake at a whim! I had to sit with her in the bed of the truck when we picked her up for "company" and I knew I would not finish this journey alive. She ignored me as we bounced along the desert to a point the road gave out to a wash too deep to cross and we had to walk. My now dusty-laden sweat from being in the sun was compounded by losing my hat along the way and I dare not stop my Grandpa to retrieve it. Later, the kind woman somehow recovered my hat and returned it to us later, for the moment, however, she remained scary!

I knew it was going to be a long day because this woman with the snake stick who looked 90 years old was going to be slow, but I was wrong again. I remember she had sheep in the valley and lived in a very shanty house built into the side of the hill half buried in the rock. She proved immediately too much for my teen legs and in no time we were all soon trailing far behind in her seeming dash up the valley. We finally caught up to her when she stopped at the first panel rock of a man appearing to flail his arms and legs with fingers open. That scared me less than her apparent lack of any hard breathing and excitement explaining this was the start of the site. Over two miles of grueling uphill races pursued, chasing her to each new site. I lost interest in the central sites just worrying about surviving this trip and keeping my portrayed tough appearance intact. I remember one rock with writing that she said water ran over the symbols when it rained, but that was it. She wore a cape of sorts, like a large dingy shawl covering her body, which apparently shaded and kept her cool, as I remember I saw no sweat from her through my salt-burned eyes. For the most part I was uninterested until we came to the upper large panel site. Here was our last rock to visit. She called it the "Dead King Rock," matching her words to an image of a large upside down male body with no head and many amazing symbols surrounding the entire rock.

Photo 3 - Photo by author of the Giant's Dead King rock described in my story.

She said the giants buried their king and this is the story. I was hooked for life the second I laid eyes on this rock!

She captivated my curiosity with legends of giant red-headed whites here from long ago that they called the ancient Si-Te-Ca and the fact that they wrote the symbols, not the Indians. She told us that a group of three giants were encountered by her while they were traveling not far from here heading back toward Walker Lake direction, leaving the mountain pass just a half mile behind them. (This story could have been referring to a story from her mother, I could not understand her completely.) They spotted three giants walking toward the very gap they exited on their way into this area. Everyone dropped to the ground behind some brush as they watched the giants move to their left about one mile away. She asked her mom why they were so worried about the three, since in their group of women and children, there were mostly armed warriors and the group totaled thirteen. The mother told her they would have no chance if they were spotted and they would have to flee if the giants turned. She told her, "Look at them, they are to be given as much room as you can give them, they are vicious and will eat you!" They waited, crouched and hidden, until well after the giants entered the canyon and disappeared and their immense height was visible even from that distance, carrying noticeably long spears. Then she was terrified forever of them and never seen one again.

Background

While enlisted in the United States Air Force, I conducted old school Morse Code and learned fundamentals in cryptology. Since morse code is a very low power capable communications system, the signal sent can be heard by anyone listening to that frequency around the world. The act of encrypting the message was vital, so it could not be read by an enemy. The messages were sent by scrambling the language into what seemed to be gibberish. There wasn't a secret key used to break the sequence of numbers and letters to keep it confidential as one might think. The enemy is constantly attempting to crack that key, which led to the ongoing struggle of both sides continually adapting and changing the code and keys. This is what is known as cryptology. Cryptology was used probably since the beginning of the first hiding spot used by man.

Basic Code

You must be able to find your hiding place, and your family must be able to find it in your absence, yet others should not know this information. So a simple scratch written on the other side of a canyon, if drawn, would cause deception by means of geographic location distance and thus deception. While at the same time, for someone who knows the symbol, points the way to those who "had the key" knowledge that the mark was actually across the wash from the hiding spot. There is much sharing ability in this first Universal Language (UL), but there still is deception built in. Without knowing the basic "keys," teaching the symbols are useless, as most have been for the last thousand years.

Such simple keys can be a Spartan Skytale code stick where the message had to be written on a flexible surface and wrapped around a certain-sized stick and then sent with just the surface by courier to another wielding the same stick thickness.

My job fascinated me as secret codes were being sent from foreign military personnel who knew I was listening in. Seeing the colossal amounts of unrecognizable jumble of letters and numbers line out in front of me, page after page, lead me to read much on the topics of historical decipherment of codes. Codes documented in literature were mostly wartime codes, like Germany's Enigma Machine code, invented for business correspondence originally and acquired for war use, it was unrivaled in it's complexity. Literally millions of combinations of outcomes could be generated for every single letter in the sequence, so simply put, without the updated key mechanical wheels needed to be placed in the machine you typed the code into to get the true letter or number out of it, you could never read it. Germany, like Japan, was so sure of this, neither country changed their codes through much of the entire war. They were both wrong! Just weeks before Poland was taken by Germany, they showed England they had in fact broke some of the code concepts of the Enigma and were reading German communications. They turned over the machines before being captured and even after deadly torture by the Nazis never gave up that they had done it, saving many lives in the war in their sacrifices. A code is only as good as its key, and usually not for very long. A code decipherment is only as good as the secret kept that a decipherment has happened. In espionage, knowledge of the enemy knowing your codes means immediate change of those codes.

I continued to think in that frame of mind when I left the service and came home. That process of taking clues and applying similarities, then testing to assure the same code was repeatable EVERY time went well with my thinking of petroglyph images. I started applying the processes of systematic image identification, then keeping notes on each and every different image type I could find. Because my training of decipherment focused on volumes of books maintained of various codes and formats used to do my job, I maintained confidence that someday my meticulous research notes would build me a trustworthy volume that I could compare against each other site after site. I did not know then what I was in for! Twenty-five years later, I have tens of thousands of photos, three-ring binders full of notes, and data on singular symbols and symbol groups. Since the growth of technology, I now have gigabytes worth of more research.

First Breakthrough

The culmination of all this for the first ten years did little in the way of understanding anything to do with Universal Language, but my fieldwork was expanding beyond anything I ever thought I'd put into it. It became an obsession that kept me busy every free moment, which finally paid off in a weird way. I could remember all of these panels in detail, so I had the code, I was just missing the key. Then one day I visited a small insignificant petroglyph panel many years ago mimicking a hunting site right in front of it. I finally had a few symbols I could associate with the environment around me.

I was standing in an arid wide wash area with a spring down below that was once used by the railroad for water, but now barely flowing—a single tree at the source and water going into the sands just feet from it. The petroglyph (Photo 4), uphill a thousand feet from the water, sat beside the draw against a Northern hillside. The face sitting opposite the view downward so the viewer faced the objects of the story being told on the rock. The simplicity of the broken out symbols so poetic to the environment around me one could not mistake any of them to their physical match in front of me. Back and forth I observed each symbol to then look up and see it in its place just as the writer of the panel had seen it so many years ago. First the mountainsides of the wash (C and I) flowing down as they should. Then, my position at the panel (K) facing on the North bank toward the West in the direction of the water and blinds. Next, was the most amazing, the spring (H) flowing into the center of the draw and across the wash from it up on the hillside the three hunt blinds (F) being inline and the most western the smallest and offset. The wood covers (G) of the blinds. The path the animals take in from the next canyon North (D) coming from the canyon (B). An astonishing breakthrough. I will cover this site in further detail later for symbol (A).

I realized immediately, that I knew of these symbols in fifty other places and the "concept testing" was on! As with any hypothesis it must be tested to see if truth could be proven against your idea of what it is. The true "acid test" of decipherment is to switch from finding a symbol's possible meaning, to proving it again and again. In the acid test, a symbol's meaning must always remain that meaning. If you can find a meaning for that symbol that is different, you must recycle that symbol back to the unknown, because you were wrong in the decipherment. Symbols have similar meanings associated with their core meaning, which I'll discuss later, and so the concept of right and wrong is not so simple. Switching from "discovery" mode of a symbol's meaning, to "disprove" mode, is essential in truly proving a symbol's meaning: the acid test. This combination sped my decipherment to many core symbols associated with physical objects and local environment similarities, but the concept of the Universal Language as a full language did not reveal itself until I found a key relating it to hand motions.

Photo 4 - The first petroglyph symbol breakthrough.

Universal Language Symbols

Universal Language symbology is based off of concepts. Two categories are incorporated in these concepts, sign language and nature. The nature concept combines both environmental foundations and animal actions. Nature and sign language can sometimes also be mimicked with drawn symbols representing the movements of sign and nature when there is movement, but can also depict inanimate object forms and styling.

My research and understanding of symbology on petroglyphs is a radical redirection from any before and breaks the bounds of useless dating of sites as very young scratchings. I never intended to write a book on the topic until I began teaching my children and the realization of the need to share this information became clear. Without understanding of the most important symbols most prolific in the world, I could not do it. As the decades progressed, I connected much more manmade objects around the world to this language and now it has progressed from my backyard to the globe.

Sign

Hand motions match the one language hands can gesture—sign language. Many books exist on sign, but it is mostly white man sign we know today. Sites referenced the fact that white sign users could communicate with Native Indians and that the sign language of both only differed slightly and were about 80% to 85% compatible. *Sign Language Among North American Indians Compared With That Among Other Peoples and Deaf-Mutes First Annual Report of the Bureau of Ethnology to the 1881* (Garrick Mallery) is the first and best compilation of information. In reading hand motion science, there is much reference to the limitations of movements and similarities to natural gestures all humans do. A simple search of the most used gestures gained the path of the finger as the number one gesture, then the point (of the finger tip).

Modern Images

In today's world there are many aspects of our lives quickly switching back to idiogramatic. The visual language uses images due to the vast language barriers the world now faces. Why? It is because we have become a more mobile society able to migrate easier to foreign lands and co-exist with trade, just like in the ancient past. I know English modern language and that is it. I would be lost elsewhere if it wasn't for the street signs having black outline images of people crossing roads with legs open in a "walking" position my brain instantly recognizes, or my rental car dash lights all made of basic images like blinker arrows, gas pump, seat belt over a sitting body, and so on. If you took that dashboard out of the car and delivered it to an Indian 300 years ago, a gas pump would be unrecognizable. Or would it? A pump image has several connected parts on it. The Indian could show you the gas hose going from the blocky pump to the pump handle as a connected item and part of the pump probably assuming it was flexible due to its sharp and unnatural curvature. He could identify it was something on the ground and was an object, that if you had lying around he could point out from recognition. So even a pump symbol could have some decipherment by a person due to some obvious hints.

He would immediately recognize the arrow symbol as used to point in a direction (like his projectile weapon's end where the arrow symbol first came from). The arrow, thus a broadhead tip of a projectile, was used by absolutely every culture in the world even to this day to point the way to something. It is obvious of any direction symbol being symmetrically shortening toward the point of travel specified, being exactly like the penetrating end, which is required of any weapons delivery tip for penetration. That similarity is ignored as a petroglyph symbol, yet be acceptable as a war symbol in other world languages like the Egyptian and Mayan. If just one petroglyph symbol was accepted as written language, it would prove that petroglyphs are in fact a language.

Let's take a look at modern symbols we see every day. How many can you decipher? You, as modern human in a society where many are used I bet that you might not know some or at least one may appear "confusing" to you. Without clarification by other symbols or words, even you may not know the exact meaning of symbols you see every day.

Photo 5 is a Mallery image from the book *Sign Language Among North American Indians Compared With That Among Other Peoples and Deaf-Mutes First Annual Report of the Bureau of Ethnology to the 1881.* It is clear not only is he displaying the hand positions, but path lines in the form of dash paths. Closer observation shows the paths begin with the arrow point (or tail) < and the ending of

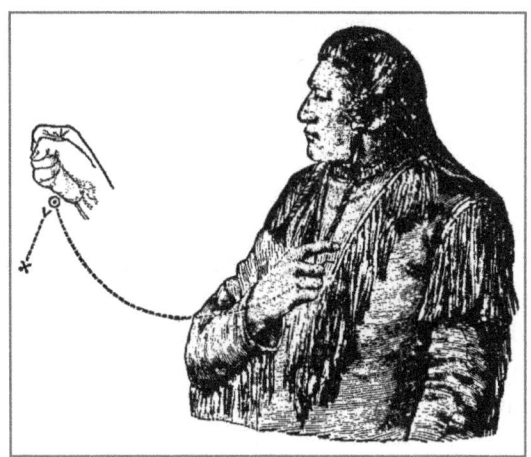

Photo 5 - Mallery image

the path is a circle with a dot in the center (a holding in place symbol). Then a final arrow point starting the second path down to a final X ending location. These paths are located close to the fist to show it is connected to the object as the topic. All of these forms and their usage will be discussed in this book.

Photo 6 from Mallery is comparing the Egyptian, Arapaho linear, Arapaho, Chinese old and Chinese new style in that order. The simple fact that here are five written languages mixed with the understanding that they appear similar in drawn representational form, including linear, is further proof the simplistic forms of sign, written, and petroglyphs symbols can be the same and even look the same. Along with these symbols, Mallery outlines exactly how the sign movements are done for each, looking exactly like the drawings. Referencing his own scientific statements in the book on sign coming before tongue and written languages, the similarity of the written is BASED off of the sign language version. If the opposite is argued, then the sign is based off the written. Either way you choose works for me. Simply

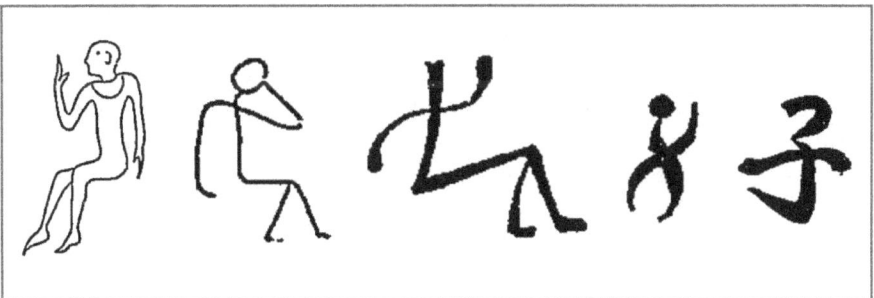

Photo 6 - Mallery image

put, there is more compelling evidence in these four global written languages combined with the sign movements in these cultures, than in all the evidence AGAINST this being connected!

Visual Stimuli

So many images flood our life now and more are on the rise, because marketers found out something—the fact that humans associate quicker and buy more from visual stimuli. Mallery, *Sign Language Among North American Indians Compared With That Among Other Peoples and Deaf-Mutes First Annual Report of the Bureau of Ethnology to the 1881*—pointing at objects and making gesticulations, p. 427 states:

> "Whether or not sight preceded hearing in order of development, it is difficult, in conjecturing the first attempts of man or his hypothetical ancestor at the expression either of percepts or concepts, to connect vocal sounds with any large number of objects, but it is readily conceivable that the characteristics of their forms and movements should have been suggested to the eye fully exercised before the tongue so soon as the arms and fingers became free for the requisite simulation or portrayal."

Commercials submerge us in the slow images of burgers and car body lines to entice you to buy one compared to reading English language across a screen. Saying that a hamburger is delicious has been replaced by showing a juicy hamburger image. Thus bypassing the effort of reading boring wordage and stimulating the brain directly with images of the food. A viewed visual language is more artistic and fun because our brains stimulate easier with visual representations quicker. Modern school processes have shifted to a more pictorial process using technology. As Mallery stated earlier, the possibility that simply because of the amount of nerves going from the eye to the brain makes it obviously the choice of learning ability over all others. It is thought that the mind remembers 90 gigabytes of data daily and that a human witnesses, visually, well over 200 gigabits of data a day that the brain must filter. This shows compared to other duller senses, the eyes are the best receptors. A study (http://www.eurekalert.org/pub_releases/2006-07/uops-prc072606.php) suggests the retina transmits 10 million bits per second to the brain, making it the obvious winner in our bodies race to perfect a sensory organ.

ARROWHEADS

It can't be stated enough that if just one common symbol references sign language (or written language) and has the same meaning—repeatedly in different regions—then petroglyph symbology is a language. I have found no source proving multiple humans on drugs, religious or not, can reproduce abstract drawings in intricate connected ways that can be repeatable and visually identical. I am artistic and cannot draw a perfect circle on rock sober!

In Photo 7, the arrow comes to a point to pierce hide, and then to cut its way in using angled edges sharpened for ease. The purpose of the widening point is to generate more cutting damage without losing penetrating ability. The angles start from a "point." A physical spot your eyes can't help but go toward from the body of the object. Everyone who eats in the ancient world knew which way the arrowhead went on the shaft, therefore, the symbol of two arrowheads pointing at each other is a good showing of a combination symbol and always meaning one thing—WAR! A letter X looks like two arrowheads pointing at each other; a full hour glass symbol would as well. Reverse the two points like a diamond and you have the opposite—peace. This basic concept is found in all ancient societies.

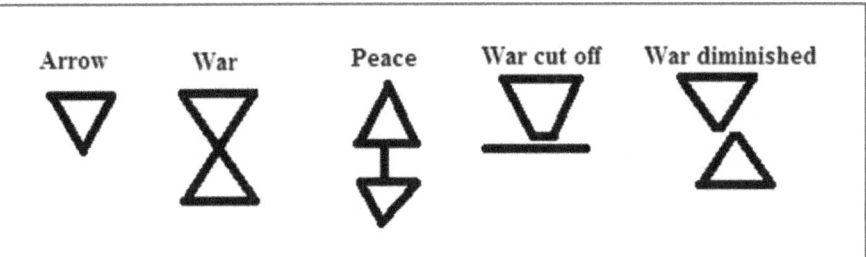

Photo 7

In image Photo 8, written by Shun-Ka Luta Red Dog by his own hand:

Heraldic Scheme of Colors

Photo 8

A curious device to differentiate proper names was observed as resorted to by a Brul Dakota. After making the sign of the animal he passed his index forward from the mouth in a direct line, and explained it orally as "that is his name," i.e., the name of the person referred to. This approach to a grammatic division of substantives maybe correlated with the mode in which many tribes, especially the Dakotas, designate names in their pictographs, i.e., by a line from the mouth of the figure drawn representing a man to the animal, also drawn with proper color or position. ...the name of Shun-ka Luta, Red Dog, an Ogallalla chief, drawn by himself. The shading of the dog by vertical lines is designed to represent red, or gules, according to the heraldic scheme of colors, which is used in other parts of this paper where it seemed useful to designate particular colors. The writer possesses in painted robes many examples in which lines are drawn from the mouth to a name-totem.

Mallery, Garrick (2009-10-04). *Sign Language Among North American Indians Compared With That Among Other Peoples and Deaf-Mutes First Annual Report of the Bureau of Ethnology to the 1881*, p. 365.

Visibly exact symbology exists in many forms with this government drawing (Photo 9) and ancient Universal Language petroglyphs such as the spring symbol, the cliffs/mountain lines. Path lines of various types, and a square symbol for "Ruin," being a physical man made structure. The North arrow and path and wash to the spring path duplicating real world wash flow angles. It is in our nature to use designs and symbols to denote differences we wish to convey in anything we create.

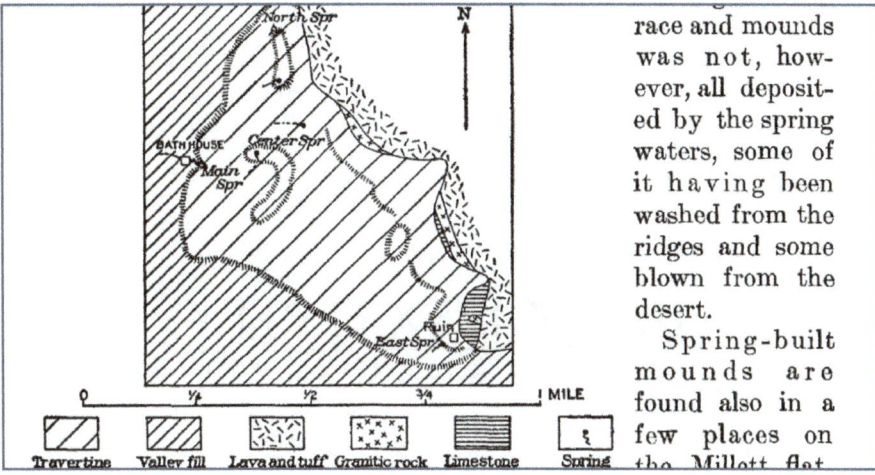

race and mounds was not, however, all deposited by the spring waters, some of it having been washed from the ridges and some blown from the desert.

Spring-built mounds are found also in a few places on the Millett flat

Photo 9 - Modern USGS topographic map with key from <pubs.usgs.gov/wsp/0423/report.pdf>.

In this Photo 10, Grimes Point, Fallon, Nevada. "Tres Amigos" panel rendition by Carl Bjork showing the journeys full circle return to their home from war in the North of three brothers in arms. A first look how combined images look unintelligible and unusual and how they can be interpreted successfully after you learn the symbol meanings in this book. The 4th brother they carry dead on their shoulders to his ceremonial burial along the banks of the lake. The center brother is helped due to losing his right leg. Their path through was proud and they return with a hero's welcome.

Photo 10 - Grimes Point, Fallon, Nevada, "Tres Amigos" panel rendition by Carl Bjork.

Body Dexterity

A viewer is needed to witness sign language to understand the meanings in real time, unless you use writing. A signer is needed, who uses motion from the torso—from the waist to the head. With full articulating arm movement ability from the torso to above the head in variable sweeping arcs and be able to sign in a forward direction to the outstretched straight armed position as the maximum limits of the body's ability to articulate. The signer can also move his head side to side, front to back, and rotate it left and right. The signer has some facial movements that assist in the story telling. The main torso of the signer can swing slightly in a rotating horizontal direction as well.

Referring, again, to Mallery's Indian moving his hand image (Photo 5) of a sign language body position and movement designated by various symbols to depict arm travel, hand stopping and position to body and secondary movement down of the arm to a position starting from the hand and arm against the body in a specific way, to an outstretched arm slightly higher and then a movement down remaining outstretched. If you were not present, such discussion could not take place, unless you simply replaced the man's form with just symbols as this drawing already depicts. Because just drawing the human form, take away Mallery's other motion and stop symbols, it would look like an Indian sitting there holding his chest. Combination drawings allow you to "see" what animation existed in combination to body form. The same is true with written symbols of Universal Language, using a set standard of symbology for designation for ease of writing to convey the very same message.

The signer's main usage is in the hands. They are the most versatile and use the least energy and allow constant use, unlike the heavier swing of neck, body, and arms. To the viewer there exist levels along the head to lower torso visible as areas used along with the movements to help articulate what is wanted to be conveyed. In some comparison, the rocks location of symbols listed above, somewhat follow these areas as best it can (Photo 11). There is the zone above the head, face, neck, shoulders, chest, abdomen, and areas the arms can move around the body and in front of it. Little could be told with the arms behind the back, as the viewer would not be able to see it. The original Universal Language exists mainly in what I call 1D modeling. This is the linear representation of the sign language version of the Universal Language. Later cultures used what I call 2D modeling, having linear styling that is drawn with hollow form outlined with linear lines giving body to the subjects. And then a highly artistic representation of the 1D and 2D models in what I refer to as 3D, having intricate artistic representations and very detailed features. The Incas used 3D style such as open lips drawn to represent a hole or cave, instead of a circular line curved to look like a cave.

    I will be displaying the original 1D style mainly. But to understand some symbols, some discussion into the body movements that originally created dialect must be understood. From these movements, like the natural movements previously discussed, some symbols can be generated just by drawing the movements of the sign and BEFORE you ever find such a symbol. Backward engineering, if you will, is the best way to generate extra symbols that may exist. These symbols generated this way may be close to the actual symbology if you encounter it in other panels later. Turning symbols into body movements to recreate sign language is another technique that may help you determine if you are correct in your original assessment. If it is found similar to other determined symbol meanings, you may have to reconsider it's meaning.

    Once you accept the symbology as language you can then consider that many symbols exist undiscovered. If there is a symbol for fire, then there must be a symbol for smoke. What about fog or temperatures, weather, and sickness. Everyday life situations must have symbols attached specifically or the language would be somewhat worthless. Knowing this can go a long way in your skill building and help you gain momentum in the vast Universal Language.

    Photo 11 is your first look at a 1D style Human (man) form symbols in different configurations. A few obvious symbols for Man and Woman can be figured out without drawing them and is important to many sites. There are countless other human form symbols and you should make a listing of them as you go as I am teaching the ancient language and not writing a complete dictionary of every symbol form. You will quickly realize the linear 1D human form has a head, body, legs, and arms. Simply put your body in these positions to quickly figure out they are the natural movements we use as humans. You must also, and more importantly, recognize that the body, arms,

Photo 11 - Author plate

legs, and attachments are comprised of the PATH and POINT core symbols of your finger, described later. They are placed in a man configuration to instantly give you the complete understanding that they are describing a human and what is going on with that human.

You have now advanced from a core symbol understanding into applying those core symbols into human life events specifically. You will immediately understand they are not talking about a dog, a bird, a rock, the stars, the weather, or other environmental things. They are symbolizing about what happened to someone or a group. I listed some complex symbols attached to the body so you may start to develop more advanced understanding of how symbols are connected in many different ways to add even more information that would be unable to be understood with just the body symbols. Remember that the human form symbol combinations are specifically talking about the human and not the environment. Keep them separated in your mind, because other symbols are used for that. The human form is the most important of symbols usually drawn to show an action or connection from the people to the area, task, or event. Sometimes you can completely decipher all the other symbols and then run across the human form in the panel and it really completes the understanding, or completely changes it. Human form is very prolific, but site for site other symbols are listed more, so human forms are a prize to find indeed. At that point you know there is probably an action you can do here or that has been done instead of just environmental data recorded or other non-interactive information listed. Sometimes the hardest part of the symbol is deciding it is a human form symbol. They can be stretched across an entire large panel and you think at first it is something else entirely: so small or just the upper torso listed that you miss it. As a helpful note, each site should be photographed and what I do is print out panels I cannot decipher and put them in a book to look at again and again when I am bored. In this way, my mind can internalize the symbols and as the years go by sometimes separate them into understanding. The main thing when you fail decipher or hit the wall, coming back to the image after time has passed allows you to see it in a different way.

Sometimes confusion can happen with too much detail added, or included as time goes on at a site through the years. The writer attempts to minimize that by clearly depicting information related to a specific story or flow of stories meant to go together so the user can read it. Other stories and topics should be written separately to again help in simplicity. Another trait used everywhere is the symbols ability to be written in different ways to say the same thing. The writer should and usually does draw the topic again and again in several ways on the same panel so the user can quickly get the understanding of the story, another important fact you must remember to advance.

Note the second to last symbol of "holding back movement and talking about it" is showing a spiral above it which I will explain in a later chapter. Sometimes these symbols are combined with more than the human figure and include a tail on the human as seen in the 4th form in the 3rd row, Photo 11. These tail forms are represented from an animal in nature that uses its tail distinctly in different situations and thus easy to mimic for human actions of the same nature. That animal is the dog, example Photo 12.

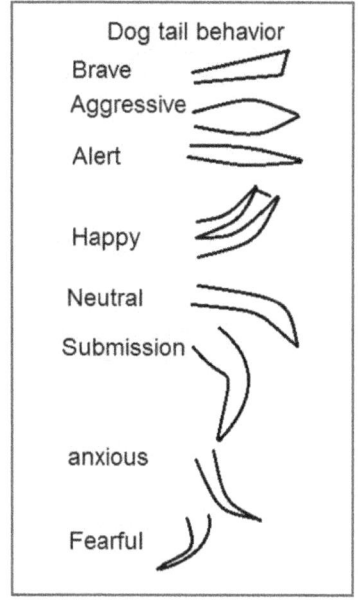

Photo 12 - Drawing of dog tails in different configurations depending on how dog reacts to stimuli.

Photo 13 - Mallery again, Inquiry hand and head motions from Greeks.

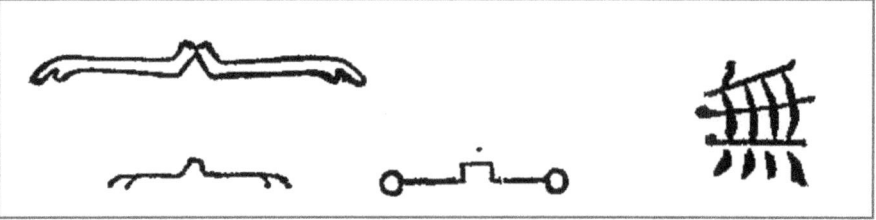

Photo 14 - Negation/Nothing drawn images for similarity of cultures written language. In order, Egyptian, Indian, Mayan and Chinese (metacarpal bones shown in the work). [Source: Mallery, Garrick (2009-10-04). Sign Language Among North American Indians Compared With That Among Other Peoples And Deaf-Mutes First Annual Report of the Bureau of Ethnology to the ... ... Office, Washington, 1881.

Core Starter Symbols

Learning the basics is key to reading a language that is partially based off of man's natural movements and partially mimicked from the natural world around them. The steps to be taught include:
1. One basic key is to understand the physical limits of man's body movements.
2. Then to understanding the usability of a visual system that can be mimicked by man or left in solid form on a rock or hide.
3. Lastly, is on to the core story setup, symbol structure, and finally advanced combining of symbols.

Photo 15 references many old core laguage sources when I first used my encryption skills to try and bust the code after about five years of researching sites in earnest after the service. Of my entire initial archive of over 600 symbols most were completely wrong! Another 25 percent do not even exist as an independent symbol or group and still 5 percent are unknown. But whittling down these numbers only led to a complete rewrite of symbols once I began witnessing the relation of the core symbols to their meanings in the environment at the first site I deciphered. From then on my log grew with fresh symbols that actually correlated to multiple sites I knew, which was the breakthrough needed.

One piece from my log of my first compilations of possible symbol meanings (Photo 16). In this sequence of further path exploration I continue to expand on path meanings in the Multiple, Complex, and Combined configurations using a reverse form of decipherment. These suspected symbols and their meanings were engineered by me from my interpretation of how the symbols may look while studying various forms of ancient sign language and forms. The combined hand and finger movements used by some Indian tribes shown, with some similarity in movements as a basis, has

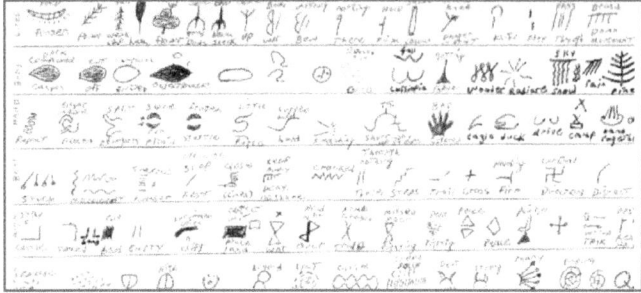

Photo 15

movements I converted as the lines tracing such movement paths shown above. Some very well exact other symbol groups I know, which have different meaning and thus may be completely ruled out someday, but for now it stands as a great representation of what I mean by so many meanings of the path symbol for you to ponder. Number wise, the path symbol is used greatly and thus in one form or another represents much in the Universal Language.

Photo 16 is one of many lists I compiled in my log while doing research strictly using forms of sign language and how the body movements could possibly be drawn into symbol form to represent a meaning. How many are proven out? One so far! The Excite symbol group appears to be correct to date, which uses the flat hand in front of you at low torso level with semi open fingers, palm up and where one moved his hand upward while waving

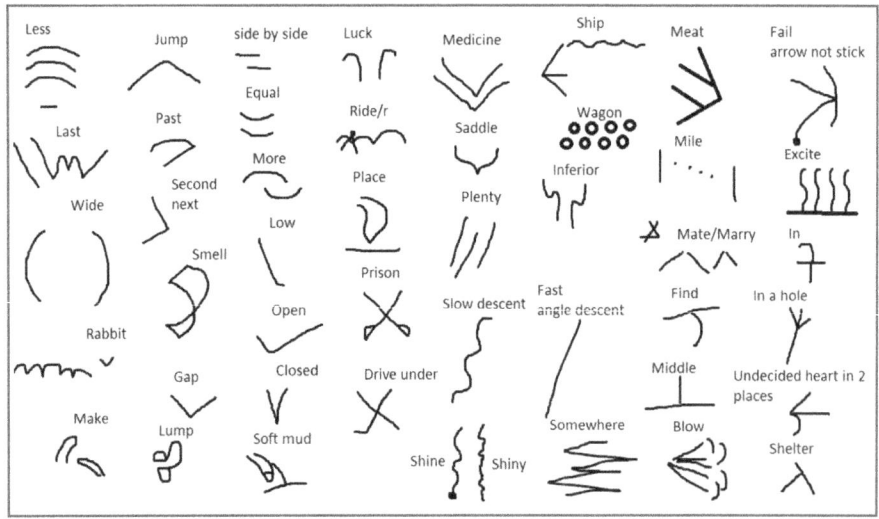

Photo 16

it slightly back and forth while doing so to indicate "excitement." Every other one has either not been discovered in the field or is still undecided upon. Most of these are strictly Path symbols and thus fall into a vast arena of differing meanings.

Hand Movement

Basic ancient petroglyph language is partially comprised of Sign Language. Ancient sign language is based off of nature and the body's natural movements controlled by the brains thought process to convey meaning using what body parts you have that the intended audience can observe movements would primarily come from the hands and arms, then the torso, head and expression. It must first be taught in sign language that all human conceptual understanding by visual means mixed with sound, expression, body gestures, and lastly some learned movements designated for specific explanations. These are easier if the movements smoothly follow natural gestures easily mimicked by the human body. The easiest way to complete this task the fastest is of course just point with your index finger of your hand! It feels natural, it is natural, and your brain is so accurate using this technique it can angle your finger to amazing accuracy no matter where you hold your hand out, even out of alignment with your eyes to the object. This is an amazing capability and has obviously required usage for primitive survival of our species. Any viewer can instantly know what you are trying to convey with no words. We use this sign language so much every day, we are actually skilled at it and teach through society many types of movements for different reactions you are trying to emphasize! Think of when you hold open the palms of your hands in front of you with fingers open in a display of "nothing in my hands" when you emphasize physically a question you ask someone on a topic you're trying to gather an answer on or answering someone with a "I don't know" reply.

Your body automatically emphasizes your reply without you sometimes even having to state you don't know. Your body is asking for a mental filing of knowledge duplicated in a physical sense of putting something in your hands by outreaching them to show your brain does not know the answer and looking for a handout of knowledge. This is an interesting gesture from your brain to represent a non-physical request or response into a physical act by your body's reaction. Your brain relates not knowing an answer as emptiness, just the same as your empty hands void of a physical substance. It knows someone cannot see in your head so the hands having nothing in them are something a viewer could see. Your brain is projecting physically from your body to ASSIST the viewer what you know. This shows a natural act of wanting to communicate with others.

You are using sign language passed on by everyone around you, but why? Why can't you just state it? Because your brain is not confined to just a tongue, it utilizes all of you all the time. First sign started from the most basic gestures and our hands are most able to do these gestures. Your face would get tired only gesturing and use extra energy. Your brain realizes

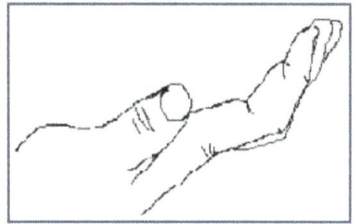

Photo 17 - Core "Holding" Symbol

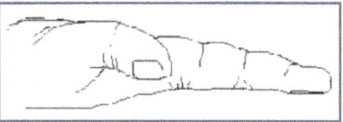

Photo 18 - Core "Nothing There" Symbol

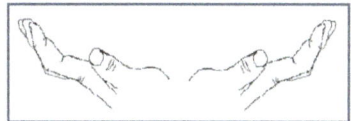

Photo 19 - Core "I Don't Know" Symbol

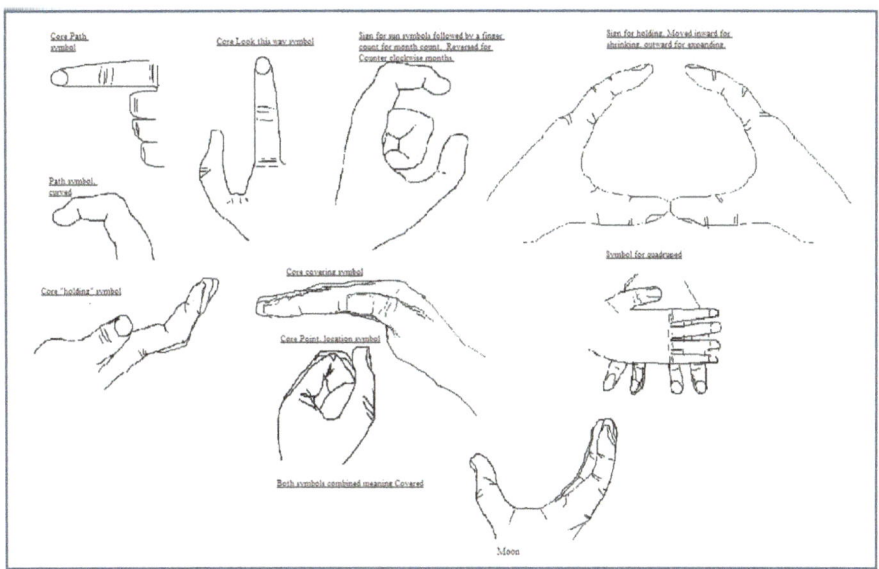

Photo 20 - Hand configurations drawn by Author to show some symbol relation to sign language hand configurations.

this and instead uses your hands as they are the best able to perform so many articulations. So naturally sign language began using mostly hand gestures, then it was mixed with arm movements to move your hands into positions and directions to further compound movement. Using the least amount of energy allows signing ability to increase many fold. Some movements can be incorporated with lesser movements of the torso, head and facial expressions.

About one third of ancient writing is based off these two raw symbols. You also learned the first connection of the two. Your fingers thin length is a "Path." The tip of your finger is the "Point." You used it to show the physical path to an object, and in actuality your brain can easily guide and understand that your finger is shorter than the path, but that the tip of your finger is closest of your body to the object and therefore designates your fingertip as the object location. Thus making the simple combination of the path extending from your eye to the object location designated as the single point! The dot at the ending represents a very physical object, whereas the path is an imaginary line generated from your eye to the object. Path is then simply movement! A dot is more simply a physical location and "first" as it is the first part and

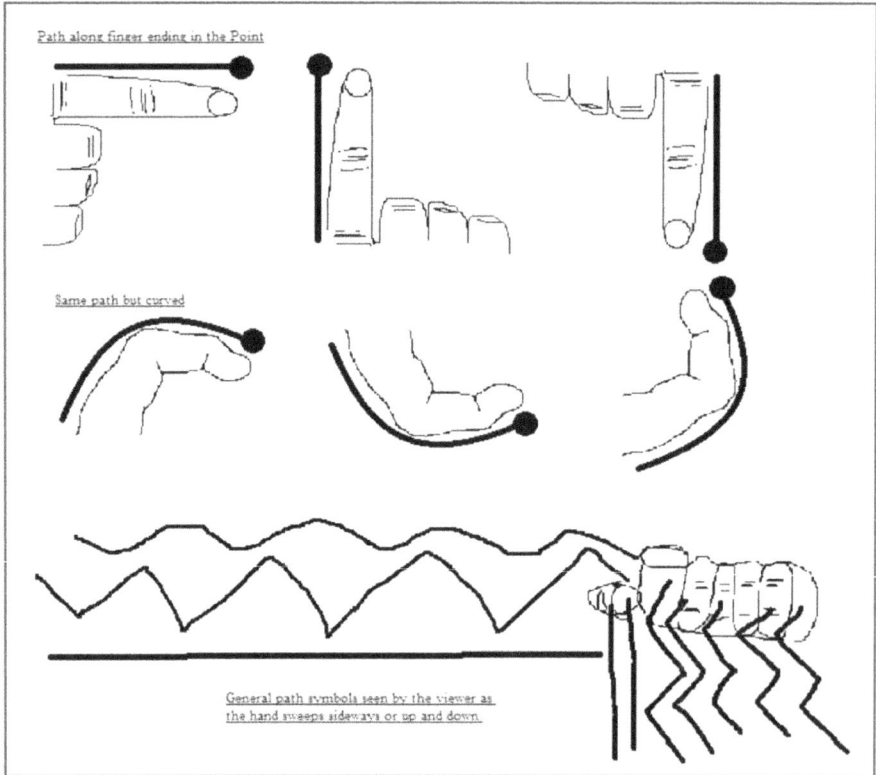

Photo 21 - Plate Finger Path and Point Diagram

closest part of the finger to you when in sign talk. Being opposites makes the writing system usable as all things human are physical or stationary and/or seen in movement. Just point at somebody to know how they take it! The "path" along your finger is not an issue, but the end of your finger closest to their nose is surely the object they object to you aiming at them! Of course a path like a highway can be a physical object, and a point can be other than a physical object. They can even be both. A point of light could be a star and the light is the topic, which has no human physical mass to touch and thought of as not physical, yet it is generated by a physical star. Those differences must be able to be conveyed effectively.

Symbol Categories

There are many symbol categories to cover which can never be completed in this book. I will cover some of the important ones and just touch others I hope to expand on later. There are some symbol groups I am not completely sure about and will not give bad direction on and instead discuss later once I prove them out more. I will try and comment on some in this category as we come across them to provide my thoughts on what they COULD be, but I will include that statement when I am not sure. The decipherment of a language lost for thousands of years by every human is not something I can completely crack in my 40 years of interest, but I do hope to make more leaps in understanding as the years go by. My children appear to have much interest in the topic and hopefully will continue my adventures and decipherment movement for years to come. For now I can publish a most fantastic deep look into the most important symbols left by ancient man with blood, sweat, and tears to tell us now. That message is important indeed and we must take notice, or at least individually take interest to give us another tool of survival, if shit ever hits the fan and your life may depend on the information of nature contained in the rock libraries of the world. Let us begin.

Core Symbol Paths and Points

The path begins as your finger, as a straight solid line _____. But a path does not have to be straight obviously, it can be bent^, circled(), squiggly~, dashed ----, reversed], arced(, turned[], flowing~~, crooked/, equal=,bumpy^^^^^, wavy~~~~, thick- and thin-. So everything drawn can be a path! Except a DOT- the POINT. A point is the physical spot the path starts, ends, jumps to, or doesn't include the path at all. But in every path there is a point or two because it has a start and an end. Except for a CIRCLE right? There is no start or ending with a circular path symbol. So including a circle as a separate core symbol with the path and point is not really appropriate because it is a path, just a cycle of continuous movement. So in the most basic of this style of Universal Language symbol learning there is the single core image—the Path or the Point '._.' as seen in the finger path and point Photo 22.

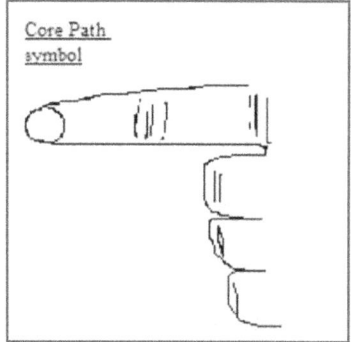

Photo 22 - Core Path Symbol

Photo 23 - Paths Plate showing increasingly complex combinations of path symbols

Multiple Symbols

The next step in Universal Language writing is the MULTIPLE symbols (Photo 23, rows 1-4). These include simple combinations of symbols of the same type (all Paths or all Points). The = equal sign is a great multiple symbol image combining two exact core paths together. >, + or . are more symbols combined to make multiple sets.

Complex Symbols

The next step in Universal Language writing is the COMPLEX symbols (Photo 23, rows 5-8). These have more than a few core combinations and get into differing combinations. >< or * or # is more complex the simpler multiple symbols group and could be very large continuations along a panel. Concentric circles and spirals really fall into this type of writing.

COMBINED SYMBOLS

Next up in Universal Language writing is COMBINED symbols. Such would be a combination of points and paths like this :>. Combinations start pulling away from Core Symbol forms and gets into more specific symbol pairs dedicated to specific meanings from the pure topic of Universal Language derived from sign. A problem with sign language simply using single letter sign to spell out everything the user tries to get across is that it would take forever! So the great thing with sign, is one can break off specific hand movements (thus creating fixed combinations of symbols to relate to those movements) to depict whole topics with much less energy and time required.

Symbol Use Similarity Requirements

The thing to remember about Universal Language symbol decipherment is that the CORE symbol meanings should remain the basics of the final combination chosen for the topic. So if I were to draw a sunrise and sunset symbol set, the sun rise core path should be similar to a "cycle" and "rising" and the sunset should be the opposite. If the sunrise was made from descending symbols in their core meaning, it would be confusing and therefore could not be correct in its meaning.

Photo 24 - Painting by Willow Phillips and the Author of glider flying from Mnt. Annie peak launch pad over Gabbs Lake, Nevada, 13,000 BP over geoglyphs of Universal Language.

Natural Environment

Let's imagine what happened under the ancient glacier ice during the last ice age to begin the journey into the physical environment creation. And then why certain rocks were used for petroglyphs.

A microorganism grew under the ice on rocks and left a black coating on some of them when the ice receded. During that time the black did two things, it was very shiny and in the white background was very visible. The most important thing was it allowed solar energy to melt snow on it faster, other rock colors were used when black was unavailable. The petroglyph carvings in that time were also very brightly covered to stand out even more, unlike the dull and sometimes hard to view symbols today due to the countless years of weathering. Patenation in the weathering environment after the ice age encrusts the rocks with a dark mineral which allowed the carved areas contrasting. Sometimes this layer can be looked at scientifically in thickness compared to non-carved areas of a rock to decide if age exists. My own theory understanding the basics of oxidation of this desert varnish includes the possibility that the surface of these rocks was not shiny black but in fact Bright and shiny red colored. And this long age of oxidation turned it black over time. Such a red stone would stand out in a white environment.

Rock Incorporation

The rocks physical shape the symbols are carved on is very important. Chosen from the local environment to depict more of the story by the use of "rock incorporation." A fancy saying to mean using the natural cracks, divots, angles, and locations on the rocks to enhance the understanding of the story being told. Unless there is only one rock to choose from, writing locations were chosen very carefully. The rock layout had as much to do with the message as did the symbols. I will enhance your knowledge on advanced topics of rock incorporation in further chapters, but suffice to say these rock incorporation tactics are the single most important topic about petroglyph writing because the designer always used it. Intuition about how a writer felt visualizing how a specific rock resembled the given topic he was thinking to draw, built into the rocks design naturally, made the merging of the story to the rock almost a symbiotic and spiritual destiny of that writer to nature. And that he must have felt somewhat compelled to write it once the "story" showed itself to him on the rocks face could have empowered him to leave this story in the location as nature intended. The writer's skill in envisioning and extracting, in his mind, the story lines from the rock surface and then enhancing that rock to tell the whole story was a true showing of the brilliance of man. I will demonstrate this process throughout the book as we go. All of this brings us to the written story setup upon the rock surface.

Story Setup

Petroglyphs are carved on rocks, pictographs are painted on rocks. Arborglyphs are carved in trees. Geoglyphs are rocks aligned on the ground. They are all the universal language put down by man onto physical objects in nature to endure and be usable by the group they intended to use it. We will focus on rock writing for now but all painting on rocks applies, as well as all other forms. Usually, however, other forms tend to remain simpler symbol layouts without all the full story compilation you would see on petroglyphs. That is because the core symbols are in use on a large scale, but the full story information is still locked up on panels inside megaliths or where humans can observe them. This makes recognizing a symbol from an aerial photo of a geoglyph easier, but the story of why it exists will exist on the ground.

As mentioned, the rock the story is put on is more important than the writing and the writer very carefully selects it. It is more thought of as "nature created existing rocks OF the story" which is very extraordinary that there are so many rocks that mimic a location or event nearby. You can find great rocks far better to simply draw on in most glyph sites, yet upon inspection of the rock itself you can see that it was like nature provided the perfect stone already molded to tell some of the story for the writer. I will show some rocks so amazingly identical to the surroundings, it is shocking. In these instances I call the rock writing "rock tattooing" where the symbols are drawn over the existing areas of the rock, which apparently mimic the surroundings, or event, already telling the story so you can understand it. Whether the rock shapes are defining the actual physical shape of a mountain range, a river, valley, of the sky it is used to help tell the story. A crack very perfectly matching a canyon or gap is used in the same way. A natural hole, for instance, showing a location of a cave would be used if present and correctly aligned with the rest of the terrain. All of these imperfections of the rock being covered with a general generic symbol to define the texture or surface the drawer wishes you to see so you understand what the rock is saying would be the incorporation of "tattooing." It is rock incorporation at its finest. Another higher level ability of the writer melding with nature is another art called "shadow incorporation." This is the usage of the rocks angles to cast shadows onto specific areas of the rock that are drawn on, or more incredible, those shadows would cast onto the rock and be incorporated as a part of the written images. Some of these amazing combinations of shadow and drawn smbology merging are hard to picture until you have seen the rock image throughout time, sometimes a whole year of visiting to capture the correct time the shadow is right to view the whole story. Thanks to modern photo manipulation programs you can do some darkening and contrast changing at home to bring out unusual or unseen shadows, marks and details. Simple photo editors are your friends, use them to understand sites. Another combination is the drawer creating art using the dimensions of the rock, its position and the coloring to incorporate symbols in such a way to make the whole story a secondary artwork. Generally the artistic representation IS why the site is there in the first place, so understanding these artistic representations is a secondary way of the writer to again explain to you his fundamental THEME he is trying to portray.

The artist usually depicts the story in several ways using the very diverse abilities of ancient symbol combinations and modifications to tell the story topics to even further relay his thoughts to you the reader! So redundant information on the panels is a normal thing. I will show you a site in Nevada that is used for a rattlesnake harvesting site and the main KEY ROCK, which is a large storyboard used to tell the "main story," was drawn to represent a giant snake head with the image details completely made of symbols.

It should be noted now that each "Panel" is a story, a single topic. Other near panels may link to it, may incorporate more details of the story and the panel may include several other topics of lower value or of the same type of required information (differing crops, weather patterns, wars, trips). But as a whole, the intention of a single panel is to avoid

Photo 25 - Snake head rock

confusion for the reader by keeping the story on topic. Overwriting of these key stones over the years as they added information sometimes makes it near impossible to separate various story additions. This continual updating of data on a panel happens on weather and crop growing where patterns change from year to year.

    A main panel usually takes years to develop due to the need to mark solar dates, location information, not previously known, and other useful information gathered over time. Detailed looks of the carvings will show you slight marks that may remain that was made when the first images were sketched out. These are important, because you can start to see the trends of etchings used by the writer to begin his artwork before making it permanent by carving it deeper. The most important thing to remember is EVERY CARVED SYMBOL IS EXACTLY WHAT THE WRITER WANTED TO DRAW. That is to say, when there is not a perfect circle or line (barring any bad rock areas that resisted the carving or did not work out correctly for the carver) was made that way for a reason. The reason is the variation of the symbols meaning that is incorporated into the drawing. So if the line is thin, or dashed, then is fat and deep it all was made modified for the purpose of including the detail needed by the writer to relay the message. I would like to repeat that none of these sites I have seen are made by drug induced shamans. They are all representations of perfect Universal Language, which in rock drawing form is extremely difficult to make correctly with no mental deprivation. These sites sustained their lives and they can save yours, or sustain it if you were in a survival situation. So decipherment capabilities are very useful to know.

Rock Layout

The location on the rock is one of the most important parts of the Universal Language learning process. Things of nature are related to our eye location. Things on the ground or under are below, things of our size are of equal level and things in the sky are above. Simply transferring this height information directly to the rock is best and easiest to relay the appropriate data and topic. These heights fall short on geoglyphs but simply above and below symbology will work. There are differences in everything written and this is no exception. One of the biggest differences requiring modified location on a rock is shadow information for solar and for star and moon physical visibility. Where it falls on the rock is where it will be written. I have found a general layout that can work if it is an available possibility for the rock chosen (Photo 26).

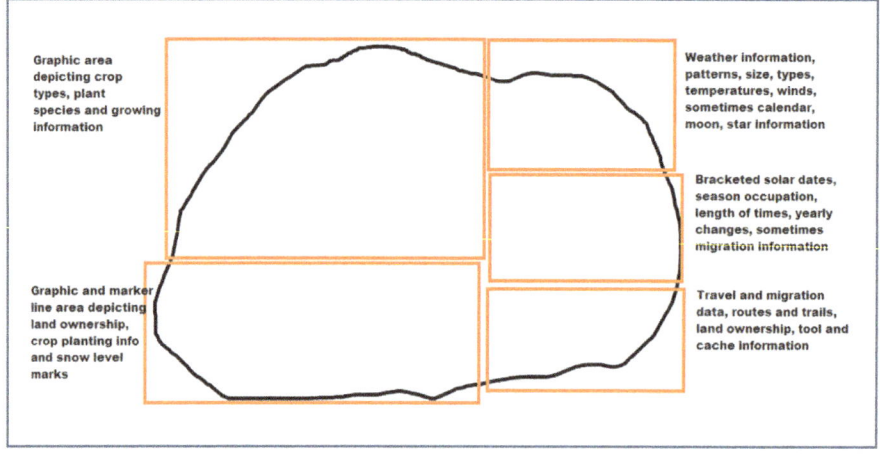

Photo 26 - Rock layout

SCRATCHES

Another trick used in small detail by the writer is to draw in small scratches between topic symbols on the panel I call "connectors." Some are so thin and light you must look close. Some connectors will go from one side of the panel to the other side to link two symbols to help you more interpret the meaning. Some fine lines were original "sketches" abandoned for more favorable symbol combinations before the panel was permanently carved in, used to help determine possible like things the creator was pondering to decypher the panel better. One of the most usable lines is that of the sun's "shadow lines" over the rocks at different times of the year. Other "obliterating" lines were used to completely scratch out an area or whole panel to delete it! Some scratches were made from abrading from sands and rocks to destroy light "sketches," or in modern times by Indian tribes to "remove the magic from the rock drawings." I will show plenty throughout this book but understanding these basic styles of lines now is important in learning the Universal Language (Photos 27-30).

Photo 27 - Highway 50, Hickison Pass scratching symbol groups

Photo 28 - Sketch lines for defining a panel prior to carving

Photo 29 - Shadow lines

Photo 30 - Scratches from obliterating a sketch

Types of Media Dictate Types of Symbol Creation

There has been much research through the decades academically and by governments trying to understand the "styles" of petroglyph writing, settling instead to put each into categories. In actuality the styles were used whenever a glyph demanded the differences. Deep carved symbols are made to emphasis the story, sometimes just because proper contrast or weak rock prevails, But every single panel starts out like every drawing made today by lightly sketching an outline of the initial drawing concept and then further pecked in deeper to make it permanent. Some never intend, or have the time, to do more than the initial outlining of the panel. Others didn't do it because it could be heard and they were writing while close to harms way. Some, as mentioned, take so many years to complete what we see now that the data marks has to be checked again and again to assure correct placement before completion. Some panels are drawn using multiple writers and at different times. Some rocks are just used for cupulas to grind minerals, meal and such and leave many holes from the effort. These are not petroglyphs, but are still usable for grinding in an emergency. They also help define the area as occupation, harvesting, growing foods, and so on. Always take in if there is hunting blinds, or tee pee rings and caves and points or chips so the area can further be refined as to its purpose.

Photo 31 - Cupulas used to grind meal on the rock and not made as a petroglyph symbol style

Photo 32 - Deep grooving due to weak media is made so symbols will survive. Note growth of tufa materials over the original symbols after it was re submerged underwater

Photo 33 - Cupulas with obvious linear designs manufactured after extended use of the grinding rock in artistic freelancing by the workers of this site. Can I say this example is not a unique symbol style? No, but I can say it was a laborious activity to make and so a human under heavy drug hallucinations did not do it. And it fits no symbol meaning in core or complex forms.

Photo 34 - Cave photo showing carvings and paint are the same Universal Language, because carving in a cave is not really needed due to less erosion so painting is easier. New painting or carbonizing is show as convenient proof of ease and resistivity to age in this photograph.

Petroglyphs (rock carvings), Pictographs (paintings), geoglyphs (rock alignments on the ground), arborglyphs (carvings in wood), Intaglios, removed ground cover contrasting, all of these types of glyphs are simply the same Universal Language symbols, in different mediums. Clay disks, carved shells, City layouts, pottery, Nasca Lines, Stonehenge, New Grange, Medicine Wheel, pyramids, earth mounds, you name it, it's all the same language symbols explained in this book around the globe in ancient times, and you will be able to read it.

Photo 35 - Valley of Fire, Nevada, contrasting petroglyph

Symbol Meanings

The Paths Meaning Symbols (Photo 36) explains the symbol meaning in the Paths (Photo 24) which described the types of paths and points exclusively. Real meanings to some basic symbols built from core symbols usable in your travels to these sites. Remember from above that many factors can modify these symbols and groups by using thin or thick lines, dotted or dashed, scratched or otherwise make a huge determination in what the writer was conveying. Remember the writer did not mess up and accidentally draw these lines sloppy. If they curve and then thicken, that is the way the writer was drawing it. The use of sketching in the initial panel with charcoal prior to scratching or pecking before making it permanent allows very detailed and precise drawing for the user before creation.

You will see some very well used symbols for weather in the Paths Meaning. These are important in most panels dealing with growing crops,

Photo 36 - Paths Meaning Symbols

hunting, occupation, and travel. Less important in war story accounts. We will go over these symbols much more throughout the book. But to begin to see the information contained in most petroglyph sites it is important to understand that weather is a crucial part of human life and one of the most needed data items to track for fishing, hunting, war, travel, trade, crop growing, and living times in a specific spot. Going back to the keystone rock layout (Photo 26) you will notice weather is located usually above and to the right of the panel. There are obviously many changes for locations on panels throughout the world for weather but if the main story is for crops and foods for such things as deer migration hold over locations, the panel should be setup with the sky information located higher on the rock to designate clearly it is talking of the sky (Rock Incorporation). Remaining above symbols such as animals and food properly sets this data in connection with the animals and food to remain consistent Universal Language practice. This also means, since the data is not centered, it is data and not the main topic which is normally centered. So in these instances the animals or food supply is the main topic the panel is focused on. Unless the panel is completely dedicated to weather tracking, or some large flood, or snowfall did damage, it always remains as secondary data. Knowing this in Universal Language understanding helps you immediately decide what the panel is about and if it is useful to you in what you are looking for, be it research or survival.

There are many bracketed (explained later in bracketing) weather data panels that include weather in ongoing paths across the rock in layers all the way to the bottom of the rock. In these cases the entire panel is usually dedicated to weather information only to avoid confusion and thus NOT be used for sun position tracking. It may only use the different levels of shadow/light sun tracking lines going in a general trend across the rock to represent weather data directly on the sun symbols and along the paths that the rock was chose for in the first place, due to the direction and angle being suitable to track such events. These types of weather trend rocks were found to have a tracking shadow ability long ago throughout the time cycle of the year and used accordingly to accurately depict ongoing weather patterns. Realizing the panel's use is important to avoid over-researching a panel for the wrong reason. I will show examples of these sun shadow rocks but for now it is important to explain differences to the basic panel data locations if the opportunity for the drawer existed where much more data is required drawn and the simple top right quadrant of a rock does not allow for such.

Now is a good time to show some obvious weather trends you see today to better understand symbol combinations. You should have stood in the rain, snow, and wind in your life and seen lightning and heard thunder in a storm. Have you seen lightning without a storm? Maybe in a volcanic eruption but obviously you need a storm to have the lightning. You will see more rain in spring, less in summer, and more snow in fall and winter. The obvious trends of nature are easy to link to a time of the year, and sometimes to very exact times of the year. These weather data panels are meant to relay the locations specific weather patterns to better attempt to make good choices related to times so that the site may yield better results for the occupants, whatever that may be. So remember your real life experiences when dealing with glyphs and think about what you may require for information when reading a glyph site and you will grow your interpretational skills much faster.

    You will find some sites with numerous rocks designating years of weather tracking information because the initial rock was overloaded with drawings. Some rocks are so over drawn that the original art is then re-drawn deeper or larger lined to again be brought to the front to be read because the old information changed or was less important and even confused the users! Another reason why "styles" of glyph writing is not a proper discipline and has nothing to do with the information contained. The labor of drawing such work on rocks is hard and no more labor than needed was used to project the simple information, baring the beautiful artistic representational thought put into some sites I should add. Those types of sites were drawn from a very dedicated drawer and many of the more holy sites are depicted with artistic representation. General sites with simple data written do not need such artwork. Graveyards are another place that use heavily artistic representations because it is their loved ones.

    Let us look at the symbols in Paths Meaning Photo 36 specifically. There are path symbols used just slightly different to make different meanings. The cliffs symbol for instance. It is a row of single paths straight up (like a cliff) but usually no top line, as that is used as the sky. I have seen where the rock structure, like up on a top edge, might be scraped to designate the user is using the rock to depict the top of the cliff, thus using the rock texture incorporation to define the information better. Now simply adding a line above it changes it from a rocky cliff to rainfall. Angle the path lines sideways and you have a windy rain. Zigzag them along the path and you have the gentle fall patterns of snowflakes. Cross them and you have fog. You can quickly see why I say symbol combinations in many forms are combined and used for specifically one meaning. An angled cliff may be drawn sideways like hard rain but it would be in an obvious setting so the reader understands completely the difference. Usually you can rely on the fact each symbol of the Universal Language is designated for the specific meaning you will normally see on a panel. In this way, it is assured information can be read much quicker and so the inventors of the Universal Language, which must have taken much time,

ANCIENT UNIVERSAL LANGUAGE OF MAN

incorporated these final symbol combinations for normal encountered things you will run into in life.

The next subtle change needing recognized is the sideways paths. Look at the mountain range, water waves and water springs, and snow pack. Remember to use real life experiences to figure out the slight differences and why they exist. Water makes gentle flowing rounded turns, like a river or spring going downhill. Think of mountain ranges and the more sharper edges of each mountain. Waves of a lake are rounded but have more layers of waveforms so combining wave forms in layers shows it is a body of water, not just a spring path. Mountains are the same, a single mountain or string of hills together will just have one sharp pointed zigzag line. A range will have multiple layers of lines stacked. Notice the flooding path from the rain clouds converting from a diagonal angled downward pointing rain symbols to flatter and snaking lines to show it floods. Snow lines (layers) below the snow shows pack height, usually in actual pack height drawn right on the rock of the height of the snow level. Combinations of all weather is seen in the storm symbols combining everything at once. An earthquake, depending on movement direction and type, can be shown with bumpy waveform paths, flowing, sharp waves, and so on. Giving the user of Universal Language to draw limitless types of information of shake and movement of anything with fair detail to include counts and times of that movement or re-occurrences.

Photo 37 is a site where a small cave hidden to the right of this panel. Located beside a human form (A) you can obviously see in a Blocking

Photo 37 - Pointing at cave

position (E) and (D) with his left hand (B) pointing down directly at the small ceremonial cave. Notice the figure is looking toward cave (C) and scratched only. It is simply a quick symbol drawn and not some kind of petroglyph "form" or "Style."

Rain into Ice

The specific instance of turning liquid water in the form of rain into ice in symbol form is an educational look into Universal Language ability to adapt a Core set of symbols to mean both the same thing as it did and to also mean something beyond the basic designation related to the core value, like rain and ice, both being water but in different states.

The neat thing with the frozen symbol is the symbol of a generic outline of a ponds surface and bottom (curved) to also be the containment lines for the interior water path lines. Thus the symbol group uses the least amount of written design to get across the meaning.

The fact that the frozen symbol group does not designate using captured flowing water like a spring's curving path is highly relevant as the flowing curves would mean captured water able to move (in other words it would then mean a lake and not ice). Straight, and usually vertical only, lines like rain show a more fixed still adjustment compared to the slightly curved rain paths usually seen in panels. A more vertical rain path always designates the ability of the storm to sustain continuous, rain over a period of time whereby ever increasing angle of rain drop path lines shows the tendency of storm movement. As does that bent angle of the rain paths designate increased winds, blowing the rain sideways, and since both natural events are present in a moving of the storm and the speed of the movement, both are another flexibility and

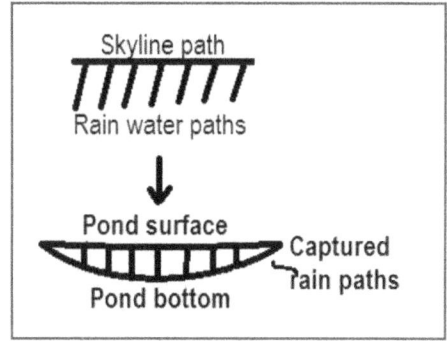

Photo 38 - Water and ice renditions

harmony of Universal Language to designate multiple natural happenings at the same time with just a single drawn symbol! We could go on to include the lengths of the rain paths and the frozen pond for more or less water and more or less surface of the water in a flooding state, but suffice to say the ICE symbol group is the perfect teaching item to show the flexibility of Universal Language drawing variation from the core value to more complex meanings, yet in the purest sense still means the core definition.

CIRCLES

The circle (Photo 36) is the last path iteration. Core symbol, being more complex and is a looping path, having no start or end. It represents "captured" and held in place. Like the core path along the straightened finger and the fingers end, the circle is a continuation of that theme. The path simply converges using the fingertip and the thumb tip touching each other in a "pinching" manner (to grasp and contain) against each other to hold something. This is the core sign for the circle symbol. Unlike the solid form point symbol, the circle is more open, but remains round to show the path existing around the circumference of the touching points of the finger and thumb. Meaning in the core sense "to hold", "hold here" and "held in place" the basic meanings focus around the natural grasping of the finger and thumb. Very different in meaning, the point symbol with the meaning First and Start or starting point, but not being constrained, the circle designating the act of being held, but alone can once again mean the physical form such as a camp or the moon.

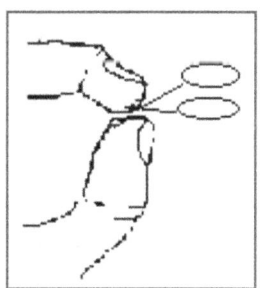

Photo 39 - Three core symbols

To sum up the differences of the three core types you can now see that all three come from the finger alone. From these spread out around one third of the Universal Language. Like pronunciations of Latin varies, the basic sound still matches the alphabetic symbol and is tied to it just like Universal Language. The fingers length represents the path, an open flowing direction of travel. The tip of the finger is the end of the path and thus the point designates a physical location, able to be an ending point, a starting point and thus a designator usable as "First" (beginning). The circle represents the fingers ability to Hold and thus is representing holding something physical. The expanded representation can then be used to show a physical object and thus can designate an object. All three symbols thus cover basic requirements to designate all things in nature as a language in a three dimensional world. The understanding of a physical location, the human ability to interact with nature and the human mobility in that environment.

To show direct usage of this powerful symbol, there is yet another great panel to introduce you to. Photo 40 is at a large deep canyon with a great spring going through it known as Paintrock Spring due to the pictograph (painted petroglyphs). Remember geo (rock alignments), pico, petro, megaliths, arbor (tree carvings) are still simply Universal Language written with different media.

Photo 40 - Paint Rock pictograph, Nevada

First Petroglyph Site

This site was another one of the first I was shown. An Indian told us "it is a location where the Shoshone conducted raids into the valleys to the west to capture and bring back wives, and each wife captured was drawn upon the rocks depicting the woman was a vulva form, thus the circles." I knew it was bull then and its bull now! But the site was the first deciphered location I made, and thus deserves a spot in this book. The meaning of the circles on the overhanging wall of the hunting blind located at the mouth of the long narrow canyon, which has cliffs as high as 100 ft tall, is simply a map on how to hunt the canyon! The circles designate rock hunting blinds high on the cliffs as you journey up the winding canyon to the end. As animals came through the hunters had great vantage and any way out was blocked by these opposing blinds, sometimes built up high with boulders. Fences of downed trees blocked the exit routes as well. The painted lines in a row simply the "cliffs" designated and it is amazing how accurate the map is of the fortifications and canyon. Something to note, until I deciphered this I spent many days and nights camping in this

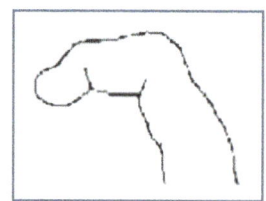

Photo 41 - Path curved symbol

canyon and hiking around, and never did I notice the hunt blinds above my head. If so I could have started my decipherment of glyphs well before I did. Notice some red ochre paint located center mass of the pictographs? Even in geoglyphs red rocks were incorporated into spots along the rock alignments.

Now you have a basic idea of what a single circle would represent, a "location" or "physical spot". A "structure" or just a spot that has been stalled or made immobile. As a core symbol of a path going around itself in a holding pattern creates an object or place represented instead of a straight path showing movement or having more that a singular presence, like a cliff wall has two dimensional structure along its face from bottom to top and side to side.

Photo 42 - The start of the canyon from the pictograph hunting overhang area. The canyon becomes so narrow a car could hardly pass and becomes inescapable.

Fire

One of my biggest breakthroughs was the symbol for fire. Represented on Photo 43, center panel coming from the unidentified object trailing to the right. It is the same symbol used today in many forms including Lucifer's trident top and comprises of a rounded outer U shape path with a central line path making the distinct three finger form of fire tips pointing upward. The "w" shape turned in the direction of the fire (E shape above) shows the path as seen next in the Spanish surrender panel. And small like the central top light, also seen later, on the caboose panel and on the Spanish miner's hands panel I will also show. This breakthrough had amazing consequences because

Photo 43

for the longest time I combined it with the birds "scared" foot and graveyard "warning" of open hands, as just a sloppy modification. But as taught, nothing is drawn wrong and it is its own symbol seen on Photo 44(A). A very usable symbol for you to understand processes, forest fires and such. This panel has a spectacular event I will describe for you in the themes section at the end of the book.

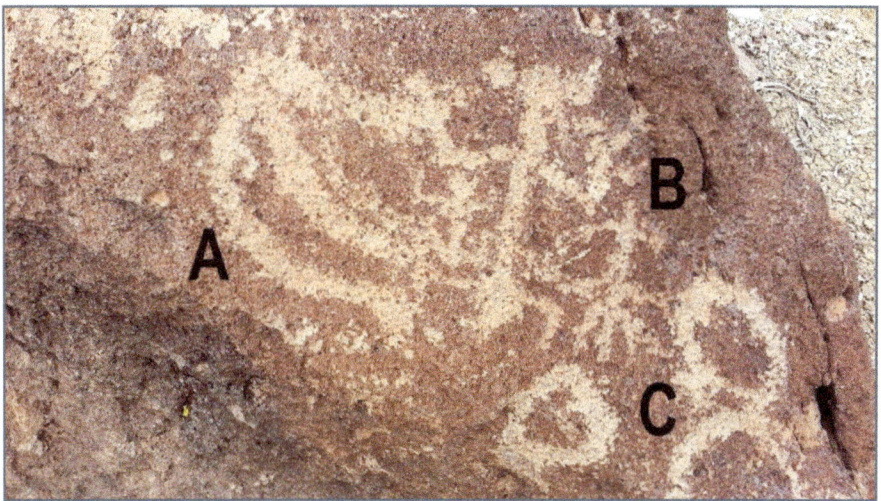

Photo 44 - Spanish (B) surrender petroglyph where the Indians successfully raided their fortified camp at night after many days of siege using wind to sweep fire (A) through their campsite (C).

CHRIS HEGG

Understanding a Small Petroglyph Is Important

Along a cliff just down from a Larkin Lake panel, exists a small insignificant panel (Photo 45) of one group comprised of three symbols. Or is it unimportant? I include it here so you will understand the story panel that follows.

It is in fact one of the most important symbols on this cliff face, for if you could not read it you would pass up what it is trying to tell you. The symbols can be broke down as follows:

Photo 45 - Understanding a small symbol group can be important

The panel is written high up on the rock beside the only path to get up on the cliff top. This is the rock incorporation in its simplest use. The rounded path in an upside down U shape is a "covering," like sign language when you place your one hand cupped over your other hand to show "hiding or covering." In the purest form this mound is just that, a "rock" or "hill," since there is only the rock it is drawn upon it can be determined

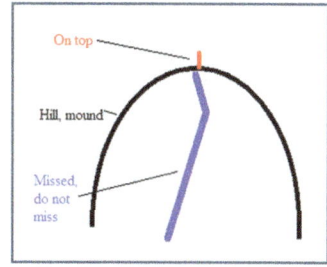

Photo 46

it is referring to the rock. Inside and under this rock symbol is a crooked Path symbol, having only a shorter crooked top portion but the whole path is somewhat drawn angled. Combined, the path symbol represents "divert your direction of travel in this direction" because it is depicting a wandering off to one side of the path instead of straight, sideways, or up and down to designate "strayed." The more crooked path top shows the start of a "turnaround" or direction change in your straight path to show you "End here" or "Close." It also shows somewhat the true path to the "right" of the rock to be able to climb up on top of this rock, a dual purpose. This path is somewhat zigzag to show the back and forth foot steps needed while climbing up to obtain the top of this rock above the cliff face.

Simply that the panel is facing you as you walk away from the main panel south indicates they want you to see it as you travel below the cliff face. This shows the drawer really wants you to know something. Its height helps you decide it is up on this rock. The most important symbol is the tiny straight up path line on top of the rock cover symbol. It shows "on top" and again mimics sign when a finger lies atop your same cover hand to designate on top. Combined the three symbols say "see what is on top of this rock." And true to

Photo 47 - Large hidden cave from distance

form, if you do not get on this cliff rock here, you will miss what you would see if you're on this rock.

Because the Forest around this cliff and terrain bars you from seeing the cave the main panel discusses to the West. Only on this specific rock can you see the cave and is how I found the cave in the first place. My very first success at finding something by first reading a petroglyph by the way and a special place for me. The cave may look small from this view but it is half hidden and is big enough to drive several buses into and stack 3 wide by 2 deep. Heavily occupied for many years it was abandoned once.

Paths As Trails

To show how a simple layout of lines assist a user with the Universal Language, Photo 48 is from a singular central mountain top overlooking the valley below in Western Nevada. The entire animal trail system within visible range is completely mirrored in detail on the panels below your feet to include ridges (using rock incorporation as well) and water sources, camps, multiple hunting blinds and a hidden cave over 3 miles from the panel. Combined, the paths take in a 360 degree functional map of the resources and where to access them over a ten square mile zone.

Photo 48 - Looking from panel down into valley with trails highlighted in white

Curves Into Quadrupeds

We have covered some initial creation of symbols using the core path and point symbols in the straight symbology. Now let's talk about combining them more with curved patterns. It is hard to say what is more important of all the symbols. I relate the human form symbol as the most important, because it truly connects a site to us and thus history to us. No other symbol could exist that could out do it. However, other symbol combinations are very important none the less. One group is the quadrupeds, the 4 legged animals that are drawn in many combinations. If symbology of Universal Language is to remain consistently useful, such prolific types must have understanding and purpose. The quadruped symbols are again a standardized symbol group called idiographs (in which symbols represent concepts) and its main purpose is to depict MOVEMENT. Movement usually in the form of a traveled journey via land, lake, air, animal, cart, or metaphorical meaning as you will see with celestial movements.

Remember the human form and the combinations? Well, they apply here as well to the quadrupeds. Why have different types of symbol groups and not just use human forms if the combinations are much the same? The reason is, we must again look at the need for the Universal Language written to display symbols that are not confusing. Look at the human form symbols and imagine trying to attach multiple types of data onto the symbol, such as a long journey or compiled data of that journey and then trying to decipher it. You will quickly see that the added

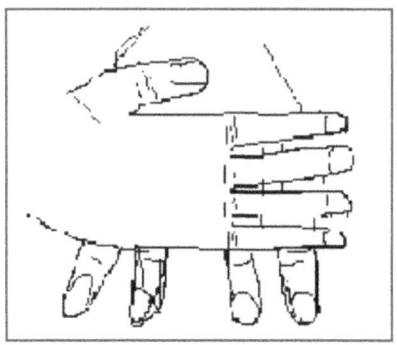

Photo 49 - Possible symbol for quadruped

symbology will quickly overload and confuse the human form purpose of the individual to incorporate data not related to the self. To avoid this confusion, a specific type of symbol group developed showing the animal basic theme of movement. Once that concept is clear the stand alone ability of the quadruped to incorporate all the data of a journey or mission into the form, makes it one of the most usable symbol groups of Universal Language. Some data can, of course, crossover to either human or quadruped groups. To be clear, it must be that sometimes real animals are drawn in animal form and are recognizable. Sometimes killing and processing methods of a quadruped is depicted. In these cases, the animal is drawn looking correct. A three-horned deer with a horn out the back is obviously not real and thus is depicted in a "neutral" setting to not look so exact to real world animals. The combinations in this four-legged form is lengthy to decipher. Because so many varieties of subtle changes are evident in each quadruped I encountered, some of the specific details of the differences depicted have unclear meaning. It is rare to find the exact same full up quadruped symbol to compare notes or helpful environmental features against, and thus make full decipherment complicated. Some suspected notions assumed here are from other related symbol shape interpretation. Remember that a symbol meaning should not change from the core meaning so a square is a square no matter what it is placed on. There are some basics to learn that depicts most of the overall needed information. The important relation is that a specific type of journey happened and this

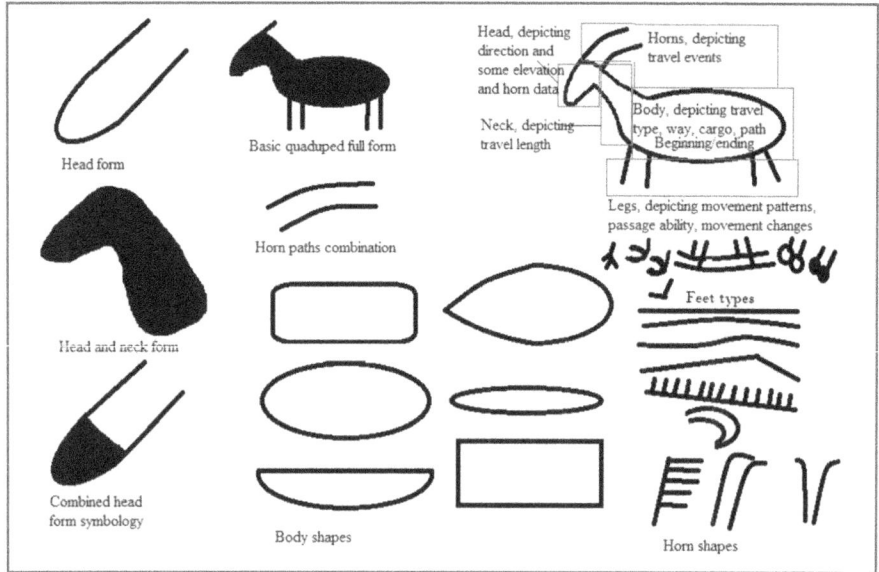

Photo 50 - Quadruped Plate

was recorded for future use. You can imagine many travels have occurred throughout the decades, so only important data was written for record.

In Photo 50 the quadruped symbol is shown, to include the "Head" of the quadruped and the complete quadruped form. It is important to understand the head is a vital, stand alone part that is attached to the body to include more data as a whole. It is simple to understand the placement of the head of an animal shows direction. Add a few symbol incorporations and the head can quickly show much detail in itself. Attach it then to a body and you have more data. Additions of symbols such as neck, the feet types, horns, legs, tail, and dimensions of the head and body can give you a full story of the travel the user is writing about. So understanding quadrupeds is obviously of great benefit to your understanding of the panel.

The head in Photo 51 incorporates the rounded frontal portion showing direction. It is sometimes tilted to show up and down for elevation. Attached out of the back of the head is horns which are the Path symbols to depict information about the overall travel data, including if it was a hard journey, long, hot, had deaths along the way, was into bad territory, and other relevant information you need to know. The head can then be left unfilled or with patterns of symbols inside it or completely "covered" or pecked full. The head can be curved or elongated or there could even be multiple heads on a single body to designate more direction information of the journey or movement. Some animal migration can be depicted into the quadrupeds, not just human travel. Sometimes the form of an object else is drawn with the quadruped above it to describe the journey.

It is interesting that modern Indian did use parts of the Universal Language, but were unaware of its long standing history, which means some of the Universal Language understanding (or some recreation due to again the ability of man's brain to describe the same type of natural events with the natural motions of one's body) made it through time. It is also interesting that the Indians did not adapt the quadruped horns and information onto more modern items like drawing of the train drawing itself and bypass the quadruped. It shows that the quadruped symbols are a fixed asset to petrography and Universal Language and thus was used as should be. To understand every horn symbol, you will have to understand every path symbol; see Photo 51. That is far outside my understanding as I do not believe I know even close to every simple path or combined path symbol nuance. I will include many, but my main focus is teaching the Universal Language symbol understanding and will focus on explaining the quadruped form so you can continue your exploration into the symbol group.

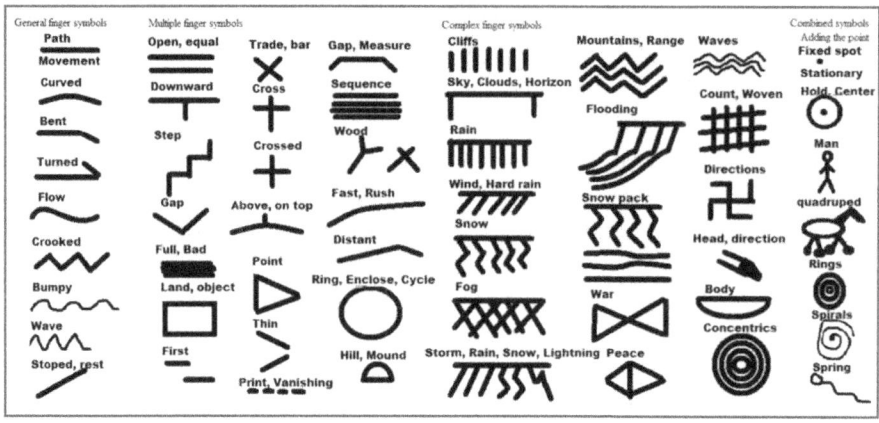

Photo 51 - Path Plate

QUADRUPED SECTION MEANINGS

As with all symbols, rock incorporation is used and incorporated with the four legged quadruped to assist in depicting information. As with the human body, the quadruped group has different sections that break up the form and are meant for specific information. As with the human form the legs play an intricate part and the changes of their directions and forms give meanings of movement patterns, passage ability, like if it was muddy or impassable, and movement changes. While the legs are sectioned off to show movement directions and actions the horns area above depict information about the conditions of the trip, like if it was hard or long and the time it took. The head portion lists the travel main direction and little else usually, except elongated or slightly manipulated in shape to depict travel data that is incorporated with the horns or elevation change. The neck area sometimes depicts travel distance or unusual circumstances of terrain thus inclusive into the head forms and body shapes to assist in more clear interpretation of the main data. The body section is for the main journey information including type of travel, whether it is a boat, land travel, supply packs, air, nature, actual animal migrations, or even showing movement of celestial objects. Details such as cargo size, path start and finish and general course information is included in the body. Sometimes tail areas may be incorporated. Quadruped shapes will be drawn by each creator to look more like specific type of animal, some a horse, some look more like a sheep. I say sheep or deer because most always horns are attached and thus force it to look more like horned animals. Areas with panels usually have the same creators drawing and thus one look starts to exist depicting more of one type of animal than another. But as you range around those animal looks will change. As far as I can tell, I can't say that a deer look is used within an area where more deer exists instead of sheep for instance. But I can say all of the animal types used for routine transport of supplies are not generally listed.

TRAVEL BY SHIP QUADRUPEDS

In the Coso Range near Ridgecrest, California, exists a massive ancient port for shipping 16,000 years ago across the ancient lakes to trade globally. Photo 52 shows a fleet of ships (A) that set sail full of trade supplies (B) to the ocean. You can see the ship hull incorporated in the body of the quadrupeds (C). The legs (E) show that the entire fleet made the complete journey safely with no problems denoted by the open paths between the front and rear two legs. The legs rounded in toward each other show the "forward" motion (front legs), or travel, went fine and was long, and the return trip (rear legs) was equally as uneventful. Seen under the chalked in figures lies other previous travels overdrawn by the bigger ones. Weekly date counts (F) are visible in the lower left section between the legs to show the days the trip took to and from the harbor. The simplistic uniform legs and horns show a very smooth and circular path of both directions of travel to indicate the travel was successful and uneventful. There are thousands of petroglyph symbols of these vast amounts of trade goods coming and going through Coso, the largest of

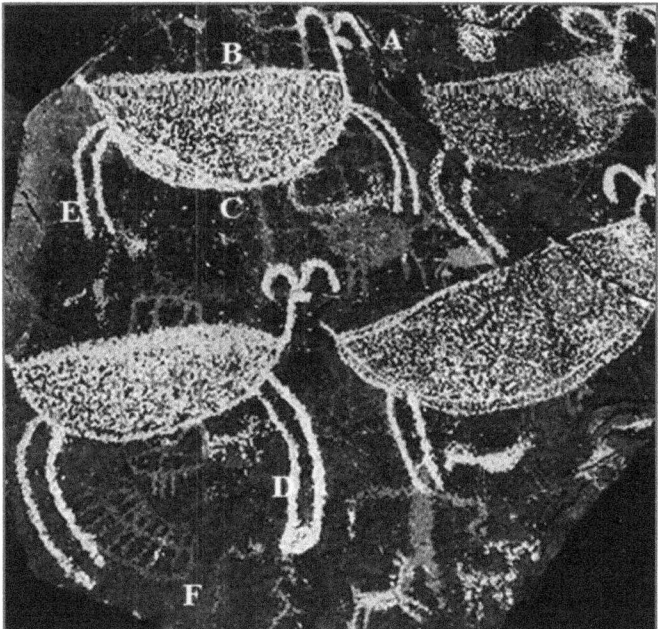

Photo 52 - Coso Range, California, shipping lane showing fleet movements. [Source: Willow Phillips]

ports from the western interior lakes to the ocean from 20,000 years ago up until the lakes receded 13,000 years ago when such trade became increasingly harder and the empire finally crumbled and moved from the west and possibly migrated northerly following the receding ice and water ways.

Travel by Land Quadrupeds

Photo 53 - [Source: Willow Phillips]

Photo 53 is a picture by Willow Phillips of another Universal Language panel in the Coso area showing other thin body quadruped forms obviously not boats, so we are talking about land travel only. The lineup of the panel tells much about several journeys connected or performed numerously over a certain time. Skinny thin bodies elongated with elongated necks and basic heads show a very lean trip with either little food or little supplies and the travels happened several times before success was at hand (as witnessed in the larger fat quadruped last and depicted larger and closer to the human form). There is no left to right or up and down reading in panels per se, more the directions of flow of the symbols as you understand the panel as the writer tries to describe and condense information into the smallest amount of symbols possible to reliably tell the story. I have not spent time reading this panel and show it for the purpose of displaying the differences of the body styles of quadruped symbol groups and the ways multiple quadrupeds are drawn to show the point that multiple travels relating to the same event or requirement was performed for whatever reason. Here it appears several independent groups were sent out into different directions and times for necessary food or supplies and were unsuccessful except for one, which saved the day. Again, the human form (which is of a 2D model) contains all the details and shows the nature of the quests were for human need and not for crops, hunting, or other factors. Without further interpreting the human figure there can be no chance of determining what was needed or for what reason such energy was expended for it. The fact that the panel was written indicates the need to tell the story because it mattered and that success was a factor as someone remained alive and healthy to write the panel. A dead man will not write his own demise after the fact but the living may and some war stories use much quadruped symbology because there is much travel needed in war and conflict. Since quadrupeds are the most mobile in nature and constantly move, the quadruped certainly is the best form to attach to travel like we talked about in the nature mimicking part of Universal Language.

Photo 54 highlights the quadruped capability as a form instead of an actual animal in this Southern Nevada image the quadruped (1) is not having a bad horn day (circular forms numbered 4) but instead shows an intricate movement cycle, which I refuse to try and interpret, but include to show that many of the locations of the quadruped on the panel are placed there for shadow incorporation as seen from the rock rim (3). As it mostly lines up with several horn symbol contact areas it could be made to show a single day time frame. Another quadruped horn group (2) is intermingled below the main one.

Atlatl rock as it's known, shows a great shadow incorporation panel where the quadruped symbols are lined out in conjunction with the shadow lines and path to show the story travel times. This is why there is no start or finish

Photo 54 - Shadow Quadruped

point to a panel that can be made reading left or right as every environment varies so does the start and ending. In this panel the central theme and start is dead center radiating out. The symbols to the center right are a trend of time, laid out with indicators pointing into the center shadow path to point at the specific time. As the path of shadow progresses so does the story along the panel and into shadow (night) below. As the year progresses on from winter through the year back to winter so does the shadow path progress across a trackable lineage. So for you to understand the story you must better understand nature and how the sun and moon moves in what direction. This allows you to understand the reverse projection of the shadow cast by the illumination. And only then can you decide where the first part of the panel is located to read. Usually the only way is reading the easiest portions to decipher, and once the theme is determined, start reading backward until the start is found.

As a note, a bird representing true flight is another basic natural form best used to depict travel associated in flight. As few birds will stand against something without

Photo 55 - Atlatl site near Las Vegas, Nevada

Photo 56

ANCIENT UNIVERSAL LANGUAGE OF MAN

flying away on wings , the use as retreat due to fear is possible. Using nature to represent major Universal Language meanings just by using an animal was clearly a brilliant achievement of the ancients to allow readers to immediately understand what the writer is discussing by seeing these forms represented and thus avoiding initial confusion. Apply that thought now to trying to incorporate all of this travel data into a human figure? You may be continually

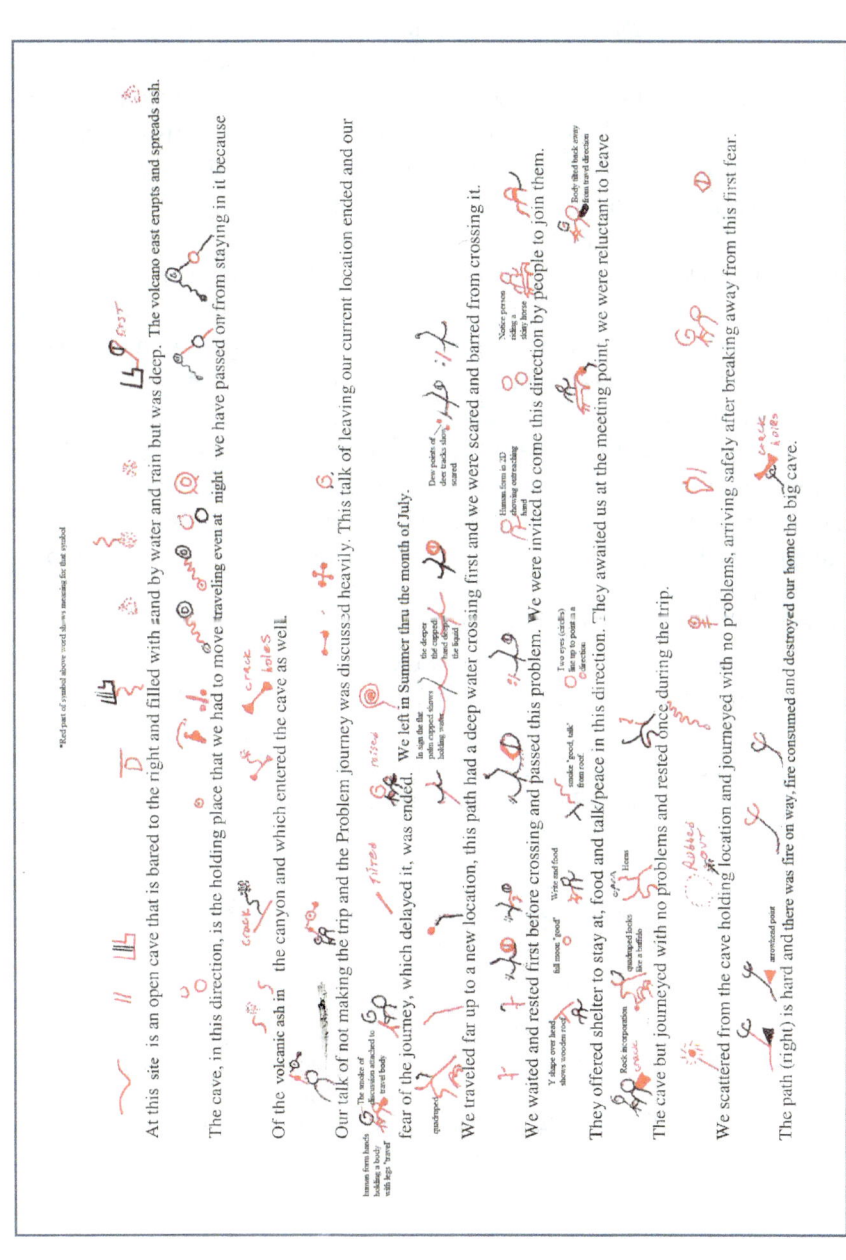

Photo 57

confused with what the writer was saying—is it about travel, war, the person drawn? So again, if you learn the basic concept of Universal Language that each TYPE of symbol group is used for conveying an initial purpose then you can more quickly decipher a panel and learn the language.

A Group in Trouble

I have made a simple format of the story (Photo 57) on the panel (Photo 56) and then drew in the symbol above the word it represents in red. I drew more of the associated symbol group in black so that you can find these symbols on the petroglyph photo. As you can see the panel is mostly centered on the rock and uses cracks on the rock for incorporation in the story. The central panel designates a neutral location and thus the panel was written here clearly because the rock cracks were present and useful more than the need to use overall rock location to depict up or down, sky or earth. We get a sense just from this fact that something about the person or group is important here. I included this panel now to apply some basics learned and this panel uses several key elements combined you have learned about, including the human forms and quadrupeds! Notice the two styles of quadrupeds depicted, which is strange as the writer must have used his groups quadruped as a more formidable bison style and the other as a lowly horse compared? Was the bison depicting more supplies than the other has? This goes back to my statement that there seems to be no relation to local animals being used as quadrupeds on panels as bison clearly will not be high on this forested mountain range. The simple truth is there must be a reason for both types of animal styles drawn or they would not have done it. Did the group use a specific animal to show who they are known for? An example of not knowing every reasoning myself in the Universal Language but using my understanding to continue my quest to decipher this meaning someday, because I understand there is a reason for the differences. If nothing else, take with you that those differences should be questioned.

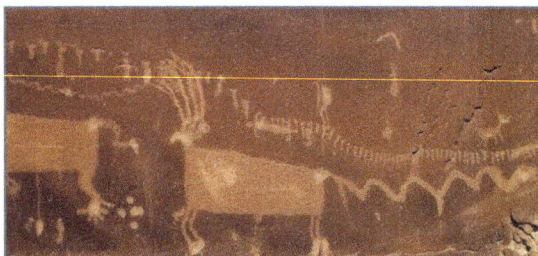

Photo 58

The panel is an amazing story of a group of people having to leave due to a natural volcanic event destroying their territory slowly. The closest in time was a local eruption 7,700 years ago here. They did not flee in flight so the devastation of the local resources took some time. Was the glyph drawn before they left or after a return? I am unable to decipher that much data but I assume after they returned as many of the travels details are described, which would not have happened prior to their departure unless scouts reported such prior. The lands may have been abandoned for a long time and only a scribe was returned to tell the tale in case others of the group showed up later. A great area at one time afforded sustained occupation and to abandon such a location must have been hard. Other details of such a disaster can be easily injected into this saga if you look at modern volcanic eruption facts and you can quickly decide much more detail exists in this panel in subtle drawing changes that might tell of the lack of sun, of good air to breath, of piles of ash and fires blooming everywhere, of rains from ash flooding areas and ash slides from layers giving way along their journey. I see no death toll and since there was no fast flight the eruption must have been small enough to just cause minimal issues not yet to the level of human death.

Pack Animals

Beyond the form of the curved bottom shipping quadruped and the skinnier body form representing land travel quadruped resembling more the human foot, the square body quadruped like in Photo 58 represents specifically the pack animal. Consisting of the stories specifically related to the movement of goods, some by animal, from one location to the next. Note the toes on above picture representing human transport.

In the panel the path of the quadruped travel symbols shown with the individual human forms being drawn across the whole top of this panel to show connection. This massive movement cycle panel I have not interpreted and include it here to show the relation of the square pack animal quadruped in relation to travel of humans.

Movements of Celestrial Bodies

I will follow up on this Arizona panel (Photo 59) later in the moon section, but want to show that the quadruped symbol with a more neutral celestrial body shape is used for celestial object movement as well. This is a moon phase counting panel and incorporated is the path of the moon across the phases. Natural movements are again best represented using the quadruped symbol that have no part of human interaction other than observation.

Photo 59 - Moon phase count panel from Author

Other Movements Represented

The quadruped body form can be used for the sky and weather movements using the upside down version of the land body. The water moves and sometimes represented in body form and the obvious use is the true migration of herd animals on their journeys which are detailed by correctly represented animal bodies.

Photo 60 - Petroglyph near Wadi Rum [Source: Bob Strainn, San Jose, CA]

To be clear with my absolute rejection of modern thinking that hundreds of thousands of similar images on rock were all from drug induced shamen visions, I bring you to a Eastern desert camel petroglyph in Photo 60. Were they doing magic dancing to hunt the quick and nimble camel for a successful hunt? I highly reject the idea.

Easy Reading

As I taught my children the symbols, I noticed when they looked at an image that they described it with the initial concept because they see a human form or a quadruped, even though they cannot read symbols further. Proof that the concept of simplifying by Universal Language design works brilliantly. When my son, Dawson, points to a quadruped picture and says "Oh! That's travel Dad!" I know teaching basic Universal Language even to children is much easier than teaching phonics. It also means that I could teach a child that does not know my language the basics of Universal Language. And since trade was global, Universal Language helped achieve successful trading.

ANCIENT UNIVERSAL LANGUAGE OF MAN

The Moon

The lunar cycles have a cyclic celestial anomaly of the year, and one of the best daily tracking devices to observe. It was so important, in fact the second most important thing to life, it received its own symbol, the big O circle. Since this obviously coincides with the core symbol for a place, the context of its use is crucial. Simply put, it is used more for the designation of the moon than any other singular item, which makes it easy. It is usually not alone and in a line of circles, or attached or accompanied by lines for (night) shadow tracking and day tracking of the week.

There are many ancient numbers of days used globally to designate a week and month. And even groups of yearly cycles up to 64 years and beyond were

Photo 61 - Moon counting panel

used by cultures through history. There are 7, 13, and 15 day weeks. There are 12, 13, and 26 month counts in a year and so on, included in centuries being counted beyond 52 years each. There are plenty of books on that topic and I am no expert, I only present the Universal Language's representation I know of so sites can be deciphered and read. The cycles I find are being counted in a 28-31 day 12 month yearly calendar, just like we use today.

Photo 62 - Lunar counting shadow lines

Photo 63 - Lunar counting shadow stick recess hole

A leap year event must happen to realign the year with all the natural cycles, forcing all systems to adjust in a three year cycle, which is a big event even today. But in truth, a full cycle of earths observed patterns return to the beginning and reset every 26,000 years, and the ancients knew it. The moons cycle of Lunar Standstills resets every 18.6 years and so there is a type of moon solstice and standstills.

The month count symbol group seen on Photo 64 at far left attaches the full and new moon cycles via a connection line which contains the caterpillar looking legs on either side for the counting of the week or month depending on the tracking. A month can be defined as 13 day hash marks on the bottom, or one side, of this path and 13 day marks on top, or 26 hashmarks total (normal use) on each side to combine to equal the middle month. The full moon circle at the end brings the count to 27 for 360 degrees. Awaiting 2.21 days before the next full moon brings the total count to 29.53 days for the month. The shadow lines bracketing the moon symbols are drawn

Photo 64 - Rock incorporation of moon counting [Source: Author]

Photo 65 - Flat horizontal moon tracking [Source: Author]

in deep due to the use at night, and like star tracking symbols like Cassiopeia, is one of many night tracking symbols using rock incorporation.

Author's photo of relevant moon data is located high on this panel between and above the shadow lines. The full information of this war campaign seen in the lower warpath symbols has not been fully deciphered.

Author's Photo 63 of moon monthly phase counting is present middle and high on the rock. Note shadow alignment stick holes to project shadows.

Author's Photo 64, These are examples of the moon tracking rocks in Nevada. These use natural holes for a stick for shadow casting. All the rocks have shadow paths along the base center and upper levels. The symbol to the right side is a circular "shield" symbol, representing extra data, and like the sun symbol this information is drawn as circumference data (see circumference data topic).

The Court of Antiquity site seen on Photos 65-67 exists near the Truckee River where there exists great moon cycle tracking symbols. The biggest question in viewing the horizontal flat rock is does the symbols exist for use as shadow lines? Or just a tracking line without reference to the actual sky?

Photo 66 is of the sun tracking side of the Courtyard, directly across from the moon. Again drawn on a flat horizontal rock sheet, unable to cast shadows. So how would one reference a shadow path so these obvious shadow lines are usable?

Between these carvings exist holes where a shadow rod can be placed and maintained to use as the shadow caster (Photo 67). The holes have been modified enough that it is unknown if they were natural and opened by humans or if the hole location was decided by man and drilled. From the natural rock usable for panels I can assume the hole locations were chosen and drilled by man. The staff length is always marked on the panel so it can be reproduced.

Photo 66 - Time tracking panel beside

Photo 67 - Stick hole between both tracking panels

On Photo 68 I show a site that still includes the measurement stone seen in the rocks holding location center left. The stone is usable along the panel to measure distances by marks. A very rare find, but again can be reproduced by using the measurement markers on the panel to recreate a measurement device, be it wood or stone.

Photo 68 - Measured time map panel [Source: Author]

SOFTWARE HELP

There is a phone app you can download and photo these sites in different directions to use the app to observe moon and sun data on any day you select! Sun Surveyor and Sun Trajectory are the two I like. They visually overlay the sun and moon paths over your photo or real time view through the camera, and assist in knowing time and position of either at any day of the year.

Moon Count

Before we begin on the moon symbols for counting, shown in Photo 69 is clarification of the sun symbol counting, comprising of more than two circles and a central point in the center (left face of rock), this one being a summer symbol group. And the outer ring comprising of the count patterns, usually of two adjoining outer rings. Note the "shield" data symbol top right.

Photo 70 shows, as in all sites where night usage is a must, this simple calculator assists in tracking the lunar month. The purpose is for knowing when

Photo 69 - Sun symbols for counting

it is light enough to work at night. Starting at the left (depicted by the rear legs of the quadruped form showing direction of count direction) the moon is not a circle but shows outward expansion in the form of "creation" symbols pointing outward which make up the moons form. The 6.5 divisions are the waxing phase. Next and center panel exists the 15 days covering quarter, full and gibbous moon phases! The radial lines numbering the 15 days of these phases. The central dots of these two symbol groups are designating "first" in order. The third and final group to the right is the final 8 days of lunar light before starting the cycle over again. The division lines can easily be marked off daily using paint to cover each or using a sticky marker such as a small sap covered stick.

Photo 70 - Saguaro National Monument Signal Hill moon panel [Source: Author]

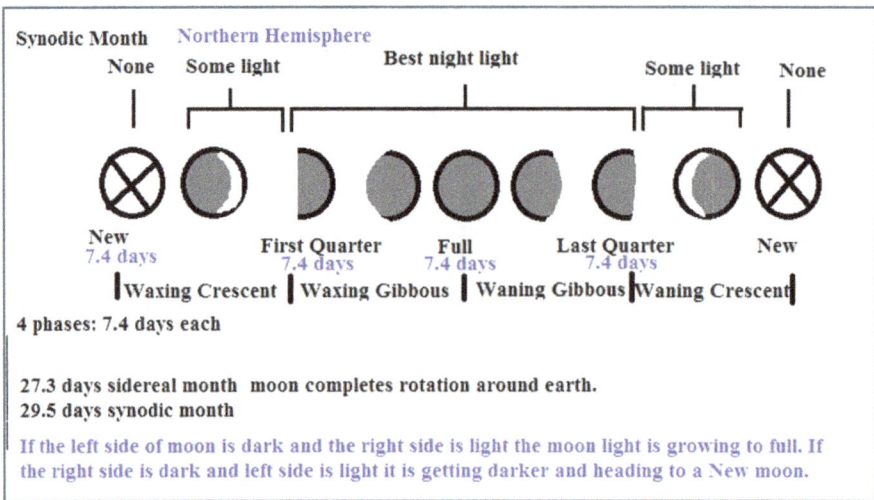

Photo 71 - Moon phases by Author

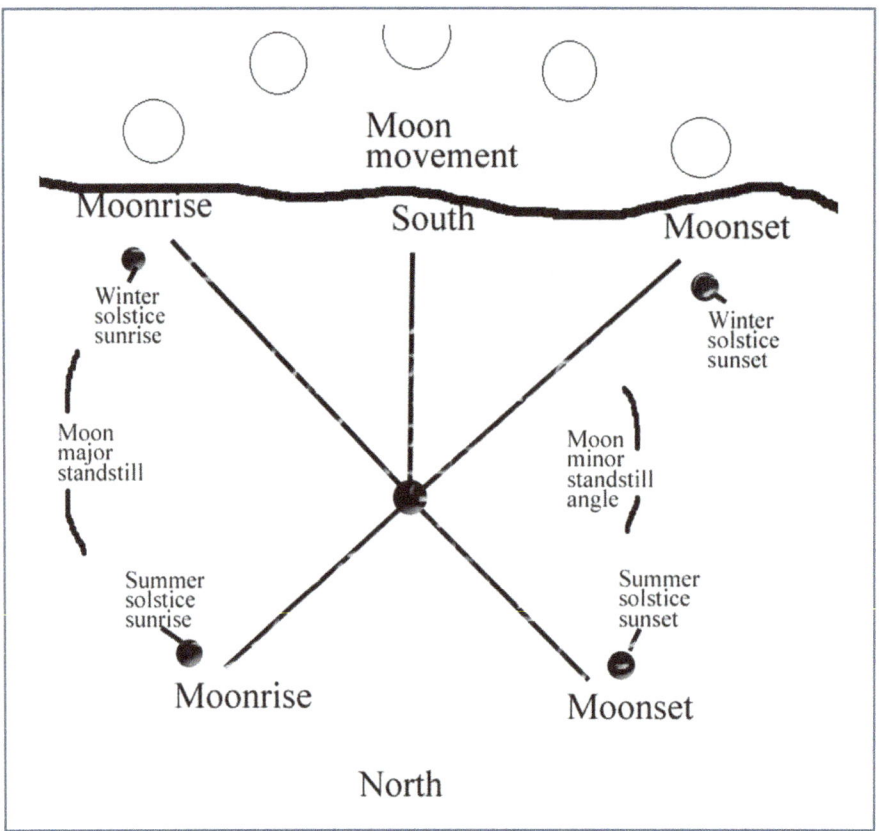

Photo 72 - Moon movement to major standstills

Photo 72 showing moon movements of importance tracked by ancients. The moon cycles undulate between major and minor standstill events. This apparent motion of change was tracked in long term count panels. Note the very similar angles of the sun Solstices denoted as dots beside the moonrise and moonset lines.

Vandalism Results

Photos 73 and 74 are examples of lost data due to vandalism where theft of historic rock art once again helped pay for some thugs drug lifestyle is shown below. Notice the circular areas just left where more count rings should have existed on both photos. Now some idiots have these hanging on their walls like a prize.

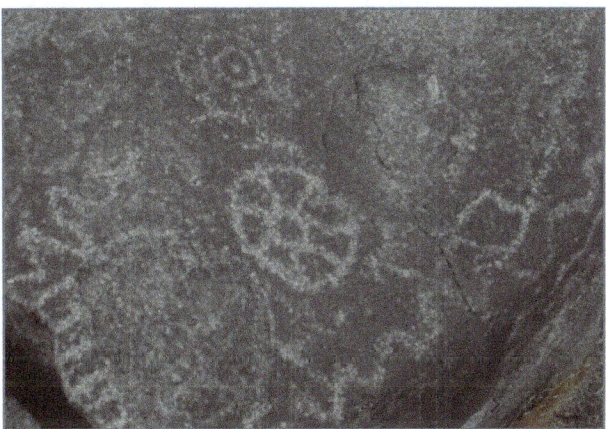

Photo 73 - Fine example of vandalism

Photo 74 - Fine example of vandalism

Stars

This painting (Photo 75) is a rendition of a death precession by ship arriving on Lahontan Lake at the Orion Pillar Mount 16,000 PB near a floating outpost, ready to depart with the dead remains of their ancestors on their journey to the afterlife via the different stops along the ancient empires territory.

As of this writing, vandalism has struck and one of the Orion Pillars has been toppled by hand.

In this North American empire, there was a procession that associated death as was done in most places in the world at the time. The stars were most important in our creation, and certainly our death as the cosmos observations

Photo 75 - Rendition of death precession [Source: Painting by Willow Phillips & Author]

saw a motion and cycle of the sky. Many sites around the world were used for death and a precession allowed the living to pay respects to the deceased in this way. In the ancient western North America lands, there was a connection to different sites (traveled to via boat) and several graveyard sites have clear evidence, geologically that name rocks of the dead that were moved from their original location and brought to another location. They would use rocks much like ballast in the boats and shipping by water is less strenuous than carrying them over land. In this way, great distances can be covered, sometimes up to 100 miles in a procession that had stopover points along the way either permanent or possibly by a death barge meant just for the precession that was left at the port for a certain amount of time to assist the dead through their journey in the afterlife.

Archeoastronomy

From authors collection of the Orion Pillars petroglyph symbols it should also be noted some vandal has now destroyed one of the pillars since this photo was taken. Again destroying precious historic information that can be used to unravel history.

Photo 76 - Orion Pillars

From the Author's collection showing Orion's belt alignment of pillar mount top.

Photo 77 - Orion Pillars petroglyph symbols

From Authors collection showing rock symbols formed around mountain.

Photo 78 - Orion's belt alignment of pillar mount top

From Authors collection showing pillar mount, not lower right pillar which is somewhat standing, another lies fallen below that.

Photo 79 - Rock symbols formed around mountain

Surrounding this ancient lakeside hill exists many rock alignment pits filled to make symbol shapes. Present is a graveyard. The Orion Pillars tilt to line up toward another large burial site across the valley near fresh water. The combination star alignment formation and pointing toward another site is a classic design seen in many countries. Another lower mount

Photo 80 - Pillar mount, note lower right pillar which is somewhat standing, another lies fallen below that

near Hawthorne Nevada's ancient lake level also includes a similar design made of singular large boulders placed in a circle with a central Orion formation of boulders still being explored.

At the Pillars astrological monitoring site exists a volcanic basalt pile mound some distance from the surrounding mountains on the ancient shoreline. Around this large hill resides pits dug out and filled with rock to contrast designs relating to the known star systems. The main star system used and designated by this empire was like most, Orion's Belt. Outlined in a slight offset shape of 3 stars the unique main pillars located at its top denote this system. From the ancient lake direction the mound with pillars could be seen very distant. This site is over 30 miles from a central graveyard and longer by boat. Suffice to say most ancient advancement was on the back of the gained knowledge of time tracking which led to conquering the enemies and environment so prosperity could happen. Known today as archeoastronomy.

STAR DATE

Let's look at a basic petroglyph panel Photo 81 incorporating star time to designate when this site is good for hunting. And the fact it is a hunting site in the first place so you can tell the difference. The great thing about this site, except that it was my first clues toward decipherment, is the fact it has much less clutter, but contains an entire listing of site usage you can compare to the real surroundings. Just the type of sites you should start off with before tackling extremely cluttered panels. The saying "take your ducks first" matters in decipherment.

Not much data is presented, but there is weathering along the cracks and possibly man induced scratching along those cracks in the

Photo 81 - Basic petroglyph panel incorporating star time

center since the top cracks don't have such wear. So as a creator of this panel the perfectly laid out cracks represent the real paths of animals here. It is amazing that when you find a panel, it always very closely represents the surroundings so perfectly. So here the symbols are drawn around the cracks to better describe data needed to use this site and understand what is being written. You will see the panel is centered on the rock to show neutral or "at eye level" except for a rounded W higher on the left (A). A few more rounded wavy paths are drawn horizontal with the cracks in the center. There is a less visible circle just inside the lower wavy path to the left past the cracks and has a more rounded wavy path going from the circle upward and to the right slightly toward the top wave path. There are 3 covered V shaped connected symbols (F) in a somewhat line central left between the wavy paths (C and I) and a third apparent wavy path line (H) just above the lower one center right. That is it! No other marks, so easier to read. Let's take another look at the glyph in Photo 82, but in the down wash direction (J) the reader would face while reading the panel. (Panel being denoted at position K.)

Photo 82 - Another look at the glyph in the down wash direction

Even today you can see to the left center of the image exists a singular tree. It marks a spring location where the water flows to the right into the wash. The wash is long and goes downhill toward the direction seen west. Notice the hills to the left and right bracketing the wash match the long horizontal wavy line paths of the panel. And the spring location matches the circle with wavy tail off toward the right. The 3 covered V shapes in a line on the panel can't be seen from here, but if you walk to the spring you see what it is.

Photo 83 - Three covered hunting blinds configured in a V shapes

There exists on the right hill across from the springs water that travels 3 full hunting blinds made of rock (Photo 83)! The furthest westerly is small which is depicted on the panel. All 3 still have woven wood branches inside used for a roof at one time which is also depicted with the Y branch (G on panel) symbol above the blinds symbols. So simply stating, the panel explains the simple layout of the canyon, where the spring is, where the animal paths go through, and the location of the hunting blinds. But there is another item listed for time when to hunt here. Lets move into another site to explain.

The Polar Stars

This Photo 84 panel is a site near an ancient lake and fresh water creek in west central Nevada. The long shadow lines depict the story timeline in relation to the time of year. It is a time tracking rock but what kind of time? The crucial symbols here are located at the left, right, and top (A,B, and C) of the newly chalked and thick path lines from the center of the panel. They are all W shaped and bold enough to stand out, even minus the newer

Photo 84 - Photo by Author

chalking that educated people like putting all over rocks to take photos. The symbols in these night tracking panels represent Cassiopeia. This panel is a keystone with the Bracketing spiral symbols (D) (see Bracketing) being in the center lower section facing more north due to the main discussion is of the Cassiopeia tracking.

Note: Chalk actually detracts from being able to read the true symbols, because any chalking expresses one symbol more than others when it is not supposed to and thus worsens or eliminates the original creators attempt to carve in the little nuances of thin and thick. Try sketching exactly what is carved in the rock and then draw the image again. You will quickly see that it is impossible to recreate the same image exactly any time, not just once. You will thicken some lines, thin the wrong ones, omit symbols, and so on. Drawings will never replace an actual photo and no photo will replace actually being there in real life to see subtle rock textures and such. Daylight and shadows change the look as well. Gray days may be the best all around times to take pictures, but shadow incorporation by the sun would be omitted.

Photo 85 - Site showing Cassiopeia

Photo 86 - Cassiopeia high on rock panel

Photo 87 - Cassiopeia shown in clocked positions

The star system Cassiopeia rotates around the north star nightly which makes it a perfect natural clock as seen in Photo 88. And 16,000 years ago the cyclic rotational movement made Cassiopeia dip below the horizon through a portion of the night in the North American zone. Cassiopeia starts its rotation slightly turned as witnessed at the same time every night, making it appear to slightly move positions through the year counterclockwise. And thus can be used to describe a time in Universal Language. You will find it on most key panels and if you look at the photos above, the system is shown in different clocked position relative to the time of year the site is used.

The best use of stars is at night and when no other time aid is present, like in a canyon. Times when stars are useless is in bad weather and daytime so you start to see a combination of sun, moon and stars are useful to maintain the ability to judge time, direction, and seasons. Obviously every circumpolar system clocks throughout the year the same, but Cassiopeia is simplistic to draw and remember, combined with the 4 seasons the perfect rotation of the W into 4 zones is very easy to remember compared, to say, drawing the more intricate dipper.

The issue is determining what time you will look at the system to determine what clocked position you will use. Do you read the position as soon as you can see the stars? If so, that time changes through the year. If you use

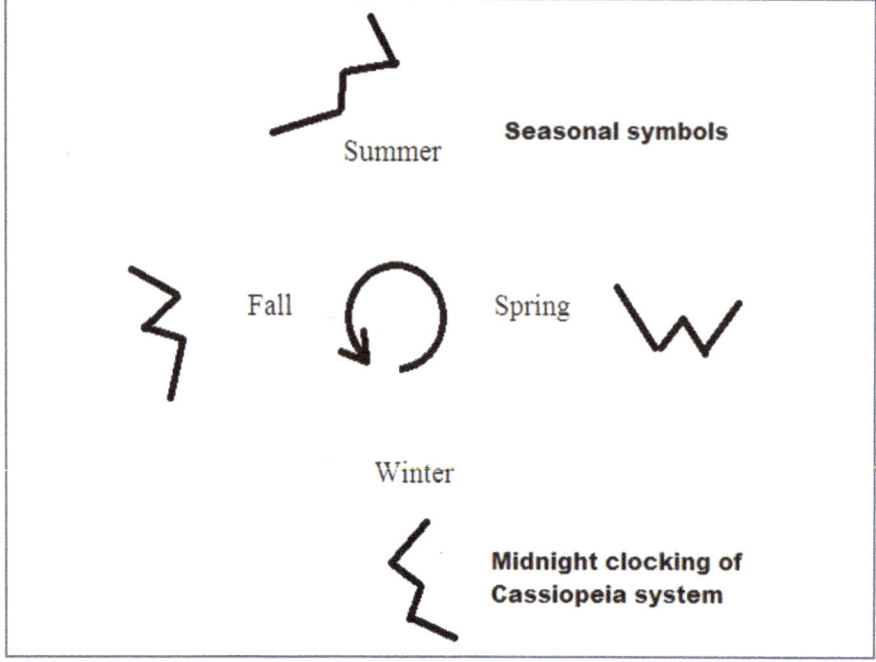

Photo 88 - A rough chart outlining the position changes at midnight observation of Cassiopeia through the year.

ANCIENT UNIVERSAL LANGUAGE OF MAN

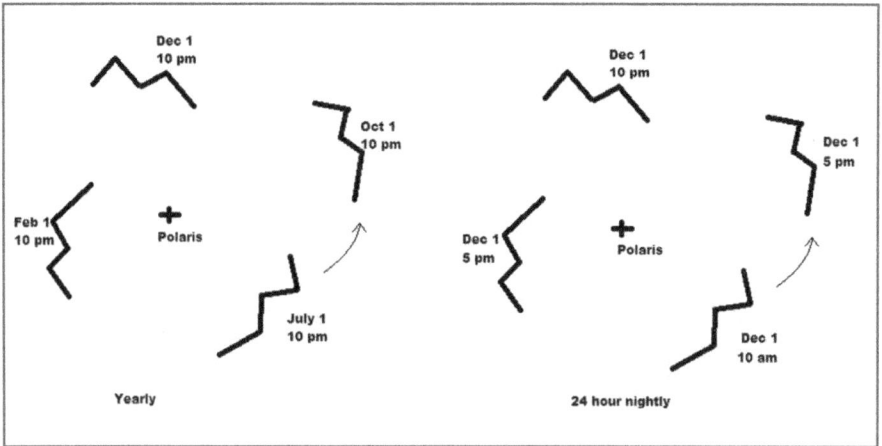

Photo 89 - Cassiopeia as a clock

midnight you must tell time to know midnight or reference a chart for position against the date, which defeats ease. Which leads me into the best use of Cassiopeia, a night TIME CLOCK in Photo 89. The best way to tell time at night repeatedly and remember it is the systems rotation. So now you can use it for a nightly clock and incorporate it into tracking the monthly cycles through the clocked starting rotation of the system as shown in the photos above. This ability in a hunting site where hunting continues into the night is vital. Observe the differences in the charts above of night time clocking and the last image defining a full night.

Seasons

Is the symbology of the first language starting to be comprehended? You haven't learned anything yet, let's begin.

What good is all this data without understanding the relationship to time? Cassiopeia and the moon is great, but the Sun is the definitive yearly precession counter. Sun tracking was one of the most important and prolific events throughout the globe and the seasons were very important for obvious survival reasons. At one point I could read panels, but could not specify any type of date. Later, I could read star systems and could identify possibly that they tracked time in this way both through the night and year, but unable to collaborate it. The moon remained elusive, but started to take shape in the week tracking bars discussed earlier. It would be 20 years later and hundreds of site visitations before the breakthrough happened and I could read what season was described. I thought then, what more could you want to know once you can read and identify what the season was when they used the site? Because if you think of the four seasons, you have a lot of the required knowledge usable to migrate, know crop cycles, and so on. I began to realize, in reality, for an ancient civilization the four seasons were the most important tracking of the yearly cycle and so the season group must be the most reduced delineation of the year they used. Simple start, middle and ending times of the seasons could be marked if really needed. Breaking the year into four parts for Winter (hibernation and cold), Spring (warming, rain and bloom), Summer (growing and hot), and Autumn (harvesting and cooling). There are several other combinations of circle in circles out there for other calendar events in advanced symbology not defined in this book defining quarter cycles, standstills, moon and sun crossovers, but to date I have not completed categorizing all of them.

CORE COMBINATIONS

The need to designate a fixed symbol group for the sun and the seasons was imperative and one of the biggest mysteries in petroglyph understanding to everyone. The basic combination included the circle and the point.

Seen in Photo 90 the circle and the point combined together has other meanings in sign, it could not be used as the designator. So a second outer circle was incorporated into the grouping to form what is the FIXED base Season symbol representing the start of the "Season Symbol Group." Thus the Winter symbol was created.

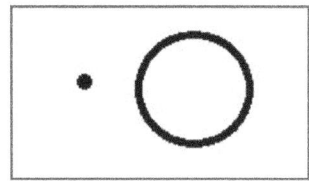

Photo 90 - Core combinations

The circles in this grouping represent the sun in its continuing and progressive changing arcs in the sky through the year. The shape of the circular journey of rotation around the planet keeping to the core "Path" of the circular symbol grounds it correctly with Core meaning. The circle in circle grouping makes a pattern that specifically designates and fixes it's form into that of the sun's Seasons in sign language. And thus the simple closing of the index finger to the thumb tip in an open circular form with the remaining fingers closed tighter inside the opening is the sign form of the sun.

WINTER

In Photo 91, the two circles are added to the single central point to designate "winter" and the winter solstice. The point represents a core symbol value again as a "fixed" position. In this case the fixed position means "first" and thus designates this winter symbol group as the "First Season" of the year (and the sun's first position of the year) and the fixed point designating the first solstice when the sun is at it's lowest in the sky and thus has the least amount of daylight hours of the year.

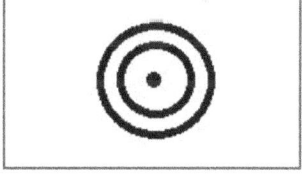

Photo 91 - Core combinations: winter

SPRING

In Photo 92, next in the progression is of course Spring, so simply adding another ring makes the fixed symbol group designating

Photo 92 - Core combinations: spring

Spring, and the first Equinox of the year when both the day and night have exactly the same hours. Again the central point symbol represents the first equinox and the first symbol of this group (as you will see the difference in the autumnal symbol group in a minute). It also assists in showing it is a larger symbol from winter and coming after winter is enlarged to show again that the sun is higher in the sky and thus has a longer arc path visible than in winter. The growing path of the sun's arc in the sky continues and thus the enlargement is also shown in the larger symbol. We will discuss this further in a minute.

SUMMER

Photo 93 is the season in the precession of the year is Summer, which is the highest and longest of the suns arc across the sky and so deserves the biggest symbol 4 complete circles. The point seen in the last winter and spring symbol groups has been "opened" and thus becomes a full circle, still able to represent a fixed spot in a core symbol sense, but now used to show the largest of the sun symbol groups. As summer marks the Summer Solstice where the longest day of the year is marked and the sun is highest in the sky this symbol is largest as well.

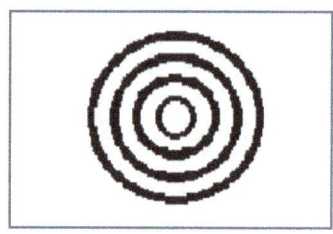

Photo 93 - Core combinations: summer

AUTUMN

Photo 94 shows the most interesting of the season symbols is Autumn. This is because the sun's track is reducing and dropping in the sky from summer, thus the symbol is smaller. When the Autumnal Equinox comes, it again is the time when the equal time of day and night exists and thus is equal to the spring equinox. Except two important factors; the sun's arc is declining into winter from summer and thus is different than Spring, and that is the second equinox of the year and coming after spring. So to represent both a larger symbol group than winter but less than the growing sun arc and height of the spring symbol group, three full circles are used. The dot is removed because it is not the first equinox, and the continued use of the three circles show equality and harmony of both the spring and autumn equinoxes and symbols that oppose each other yearly.

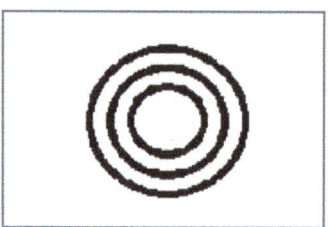

Photo 94 - Core combinations: autumn

Nature Tied Symbols

Top of Photo 95 represents the sun's arc in the sky is lowest in winter and highest in summer with central height existing in both the spring and autumn equinox periods. If you combine these three arcs as circles in circles you create a similar looking existence to all the season symbols from smallest to largest.

Lower symbols are shown in order to recreate how it relates to the sun movement seen in Photo 95 arc patterns.

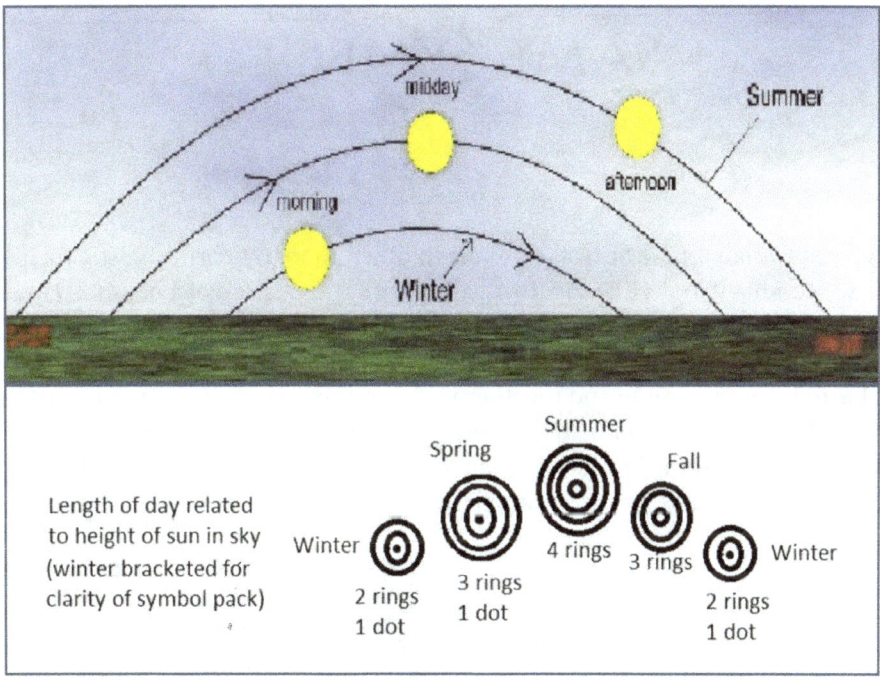

Photo 95

3D Newer Style of the Same Symbols

I want to show these Season symbols in other, more modern, stylistic forms to see what it looks like. Again, dealing with the creation of a newer 2D and 3D styling of these symbols you are able to compress them, arrange them into linear formations and thus columns, and they become a condensed version able to be drawn inline and together in a more compact form for transportation. Thus the style can be woven into blankets, drawn on tablets, skins and pottery in a very uniform design much more akin to language writing.

Photo 96 is a fantastic example of a 3D representation of a combined Season Symbol group. Note the straight shadow cast against the lines.

Photo 97 of "Little SunMan" picture from Gail Root Deming, NM in the same combined symbol group panel group as Big SunMan above, but this panel is cast on by a ray of sun emanating through a remote rock outcrop with a square opening in it up the hill during the Summer and Winter Solstices. You can meet great folks like Gail Root and Logan Ray Bier who love petroglyphs on social media sites like Facebook Groups

Photo 96 - "Big SunMan" [Source: Gail Root of Deming, New Mexico]

Nevada Backroads; Petroglyph of Nevada and Beyond. See "hands" chapter for more understanding of this panel and the We Nooch Society.

Photo 98, the Little SunMan projection rock photo by Gail Root Deming, NM again, note the rock with Little SunMan panel on the opposite side of this photo is facing the keyhole square opening.

Photo 97 - "Little SunMan" [Source: Gail Root of Deming, New Mexico]

Photo 98 - Little SunMan projection rock [Source: Gail Root of Deming, New Mexico]

Photo 99 - To sum up the modified symbols then, it can be represented as these symbols used in 3D style.

Seasonal Day Counters

Like the moon count symbol group, there is the season count symbols. Directly linked and bracketing the month started in panel (Photo 100) at Signal Hill, Arizona. the count is an easy mark off of 10 days in the top circle in the image (the central dot open showing it is used as a count and this circle group is touching the path line from the month symbol in the center to where you start the count) to equal 1 mark off for a 9 count in the second circle (the lower circle with a solid center showing it is not used). When the 10 count is completed and each of the 9 segments are marked off with paint, you have completed the 90 days between each season/solstice to equinox.

ANCIENT UNIVERSAL LANGUAGE OF MAN

Photo 100 - [Source: Author]

Photo 101 - A 13-count system inside a season symbol

Circumference Data

This panel shows the next criteria of data, the circumference data. The circumference around a seasonal object can be used to provide more data if it is required. Photo 102 shows a planting chart clearly depicts obvious rain cycles near this wide field area and even what direction they swarm into the valley. But you will notice this is not a usual season symbol group in the center of the rain paths and the rock incorporation of the natural crack going through the symbol causing a shadow to be used as part of the symbol.

Author photos 104-108 showing grouping of many sites with different looks of the circumference data. Some of this data incorporates standstills, crossovers of sun and moon, minimum and maximum movements, and quarter marks between seasons.

Photo 102 - Circumference data with rock incorporation [Source: Author]

Photo 103 - Mixture of picto and geo glyphs [Source: Carl Bjork]

Photo 104 - Graveyard panel [Source: Author]

Photo 105 - Single reference panel [Source: Author]

Photo 106 - Site combined circumference data [Source: Author]

Photo 107 - Small circumference data [Source: Author]

Photo 108 - Central section obscured but good showing circumference data [Source: Author]

Contracting and Expanding Paths

Seen in the panel in Photo 109, the sign language for compressing and expanding is by using the open circle paths made by the fingers and thumbs making an open circle touching each other (Circumference Plate). Then moving the hands inward to shrink the circle or outward to expand it shown in Photo 110. This is used in dealing with the season's beginning and ending cycles showing radiating lines (paths) to show the direction the symbol is growing or shrinking by placing the lines toward the inside or outside of the circle line. As the seasons are 3 months the first 1.5 months fall into expansion and the last 1.5 months declining. Usually the line numbers around the circle are in groups of 7 or 13, but could be more or less and used as small shadow paths for times designated.

Photo 109 - Path lines radiating outward [Source: Author]

Circumference Radiating Shadow Lines

As seen on the last symbol on the Circumference Photo 110, some radiating lines are not showing contraction or expansion and just as a generic sun symbol to convey that the radiating lines are strictly for shadow line angles of that given time connected to the rain.

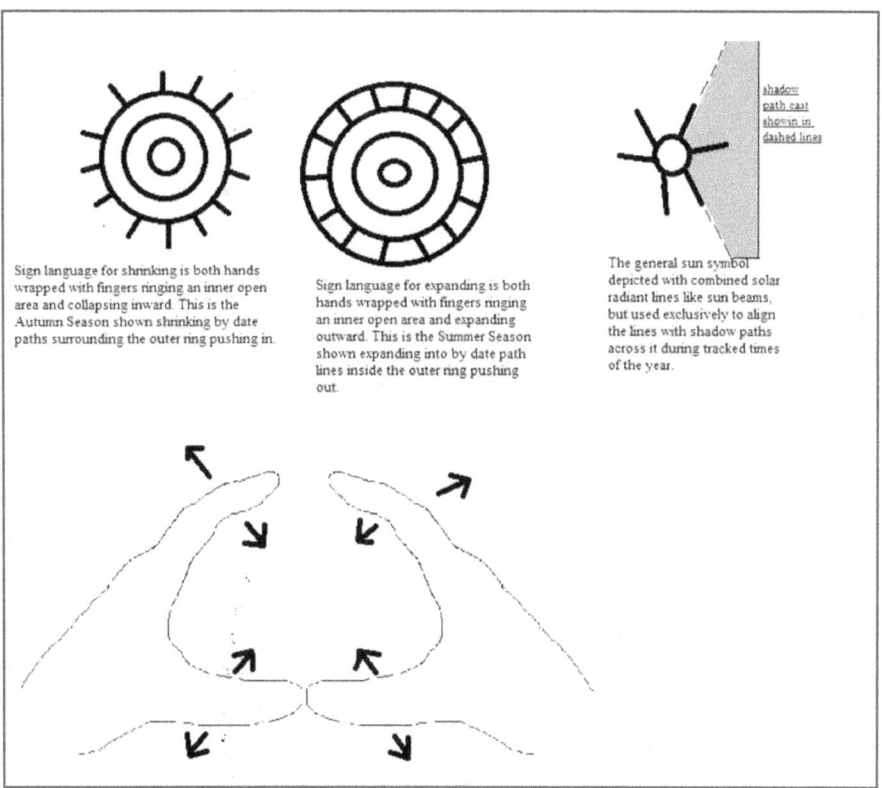

Photo 110 - Contracting and expanding path lines related to sign language. Note the hands do not "push" out or "pull" inward in what would be an unnatural force of your movements but just the opposite in a "squeezing" grip inward from the Outside of an object and a "tugging" outward from the Inside of an object!

Cassiopeia Included as the Other Time Keeper

Back to our Cassiopeia panel displayed earlier on Photo 111, but expanded to see the complete season circle we find more data on the times of this hunting site. It is a cliffs complex where deer were directed over the cliffs during migration in fall ending in winter. The migrations here even now are fantastic and the animals use the same trails even today due to terrain. Miles of this hunting complex exist and it is good to remember when you find a hunting site you should branch out because you will find associated panels along the complex areas sometimes for more than 6 miles.

Photo 111 - Expanded Cassiopeia panel to show combined season symbol above and connected to it.

Looking at this Photo 111 to the right is the fall symbol (B) with a human form (C) holding a thin line (A) (yes, again not a style) going through the symbol. The symbol has usable data around it's radius (D) you will witness later and most important is the extending path line drawn out from the middle ring (E) down to the Cassiopeia symbols (F) showing times and season beginning and endings of the migration run. This combination is fantastic to show the relation of the two. Again the site has been chalked over the years

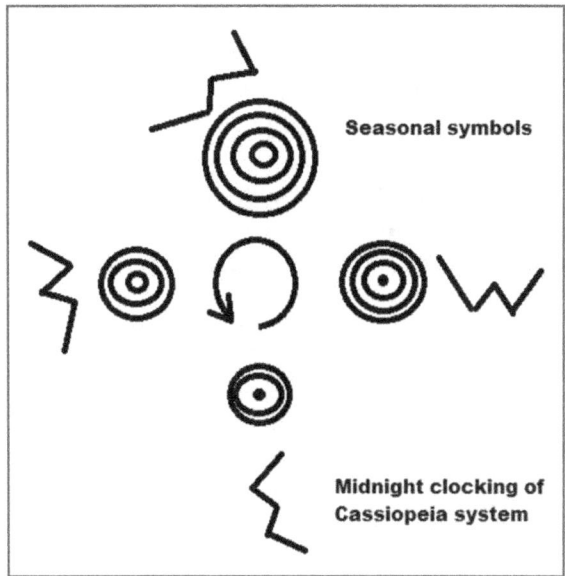

Photo 112 - The star system in relation to a yearly Seasonal setting in relation to the season symbol group. A good way to decide a season at night. Of course Cassiopeia can be used as a daily clock.

so some objects appear more distinct than others, but if you look you will see a center dot to designate a combined symbol of fall and winter! This is something you will constantly encounter when sites were used several times a year or through a length of time in the year, like crop sites.

Back to the panel another un-obvious characteristic barely seen here, because some highly educated individual didn't chalk everything because scratches were thought useless, are many radiating lines scratched all around the outer circles path. These are the most important because the placement of almost every sun symbol is placed so a shadow from a rock point or edge will cast upon the spot during the time of year required and thus that is the way the users of the site can track when they must be there for the site's usage. The lines are shadow paths tracked over the years to better understand exact times they need to remain there and what the conditions are! It is done everywhere and you must immediately search for these scratches to define just how well the site data is represented. If there are few scratch signs little or no yearly tracking was accomplished and may be a one time use site or event. This site not only has hundreds of scratches almost on top of each other, there are numerous areas along the cliffs tracked the same way also for confirmation of the full panel. A panel of this importance is usually not drawn in fully until some time has passed to assure complete data can be listed without screwing up the symbol area. I still hunt deer here today and I have seen vast groups of hundreds of deer running past here when I was a child. The site was listed in prior writings as "hardly used by few in the past with sporadic lithage and bones " but over time the weather now has eroded the sands in the wash below and you can clearly see you're literally walking on solid bones and broken tips of spears. The site was amazingly successful.

Rock Shadow Incorporation

You will notice on Photo 111 the season circle is somewhat out of round. You will witness this often and corresponds to the shadow line here, visible on Photo 113, that is cast onto the rock thus assisting understanding (and actual tracking of the time) with rock incorporation. We will get into plenty of that later.

Photo 113 - Showing panel location on the cliff and the shadow cast over the season symbol of the panel

Shadow Lines

Like anyone with age, rocks have wrinkles. Usually big ones but they have them and the ancients used them to their advantage. They witnessed rock edges casting shadows into areas on the rock where panels could be drawn and the yearly progression tracked by using these shadows as a time clock when it would hit the exact same spot each year.

Photo 114 - Author's modified photo of shadow line zones

Observe on the shadow line panel in Photo 114 the divided season symbols as they are related to how the natural curvature of the rock casted shadow through the year. The shadow casted outlines are highlighted with various shades of white to depict the exact look of how the sun and shadow shapes would look when each date that is tracked arrives. The rock lip above and round to the left is outlined as the dark line so you can see the rock lip that provides that shadow casting.

    This site is best to describe what you will witness in sites dedicated mostly to the sun's yearly path. The season symbols can be seen on each level with a shadow line evident (the highlighted layers). The spring symbols and the corresponding marks indicating days of the three months can be seen completely tracked along the shadows path. Seen is another half symbol used as a fixed sun marker designating a point in time is the elongated tall cover path symbol with a line in the center. You can see them side by side along the shadow paths used as count lines. No, they are not vulvas or woman forms as many proclaim. Vulva forms do exist, usually on existing rock structures which mimic the form naturally, then enhanced further. In occasion they are used with the sun symbol form, possibly as the yearly birth.

Bracketing with Season Symbols

The start of ancient Universal Language story panels usually start with the Eastern region of the rock and spreads toward the west. This again is due to the natural movement of the sun as it starts its day rising in the East and setting in the West. So depending on the direction of the panel this direction is not set as a right to left pattern but could very well be left to right or down to up. The start of a large story usually begins with "Brackets", those symbols which are usually Season symbols but could be simply single day symbols, a mix of Seasons and Months (all symbols explained in it's own chapters). These symbols are usually located close to each other with an open gap and a path line that encompases the entire story by encirclement, or most of it, and is anchored by these bracketing symbols.

Photo 115 is a perfect panel bracketed (East being to the right), but much overwritten with data making it very hard to distinguish singular symbols to comprehend. The site is a place deer migrate to in fall and winter to stay due to ample food and water and, pile in here by the thousands, now by the hundreds. You can clearly see the season symbols used lower right in what is called a "Bracketing" of the story. You will see bracketing of a story a lot on keystone rocks, this is the main panel rock, all others are smaller stories. This panel shows the time between fall and winter use and broadens out in the surrounding paths to tell the complete story of food heights and many other topics including weather data listed above left and on this rock along the entire upper area of the rock. The brackets are lower right and are the start of the story and the ending.

Photo 115 - Bracketed panel

Photo 116 - Another bracketed story from a keystone

Combining Different Season Symbols Into One

Here on Photo 117 is a panel at a site used for various activities in spring and fall explained in another chapter. Referencing the combining of the season symbols is common, but the outer ring is light and undefined more than the central rings, showing it designates a possible fourth ring. The heavy incised circles and dot are the focus of the times this site is occupied and represents the combined summer and fall usage seasons. Why not draw separate symbols for each season? Because these tasks were done in both seasons, thus being the same combined symbol informs you of that. If the tasks were separate the symbols usually are separated or both tasks were "as important" and justified equality in your understanding of the site's usage. Another reason for combinations is if the rock shadow incorporation happens to give equal shadow casting within the same region, making it easy just to keep the original symbol and adding the combination symbol to the group.

Other Season Reference

The Universal Language was not just used as the rock writing of the ancients, it was used in the rock creations now known as Megaliths, scattered all over the world. The magnificent monuments, observatories, and laboratories were built with the Universal Language symbology INCORPORATED into their design. Online research can find hundreds of related Megaliths, geoglyphs, and other massive sites entwined with the Universal Language symbols. Some of these megaliths like Stonehenge and other henges were platforms for the solidification of knowledge and to pass on a message to the future and further observance of the archeoastronomy mysteries while also

Photo 117 - Combined season symbols

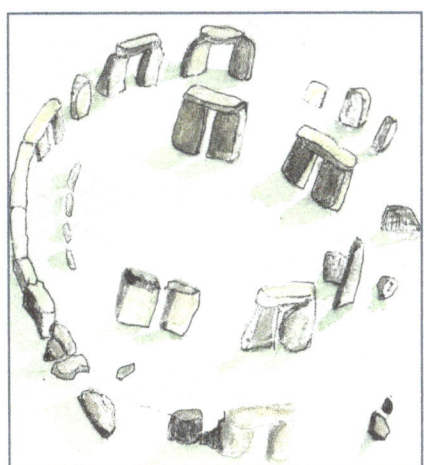

Photo 118 - Painting by Willow Phillips of Stonehenge from above.

Photo 119 - Gubekli Tepi by Mick Hobday, There are over thirty of these structures intentionally buried at this site incorporating the Universal Language symbols into their very design.

be used as a platform to support a tall structure (now long gone) built on it used for ritual precessions. Unlocking the key to these messages will reveal knowledge that may save us again someday. Stories of old relating to a tower to the heavens being built by all could easily be referencing the vast megaliths of old being built on a global scale to the heavens. And the downfall of the singular task did end abruptly, but by the devastating natural force they recognized and attempted to communicate forward so we will be aware of it's return. If such a task was put forth to accomplish this monumental and enduring message because their end was imminent it may be somewhat important to our future!

Photo 120 - Painting by Willow Phillips of Gilgal the "Israeli Stonehenge."

"The Gilgal is the Israeli Stonehenge. The structure is composed of over 40,000 stones that are arranged in 4 circles. It is quite big – the diameter of the outer circle is about 150 meters/490 feet. The site is estimated to be 5,000 years old.

It is not totally understood what the purpose of the structure was. Some think it was a sort of a calendar or maybe a tomb or worship site.

Strangely enough it is best seen from above; however it sits on a plateau with no hills around it – which raises further questions regarding the purpose of the structure.

Gilgal or Galgal in Hebrew means a circle. Refaim means ghosts. But the Refaim were also a race of giant people that lived in the Bashan, which is the Golan of today. And they might just be the ones who built the place."

Source: *Israel-Travel-and-Tours.com/rephaim.htm*

Daily Tracking Symbols

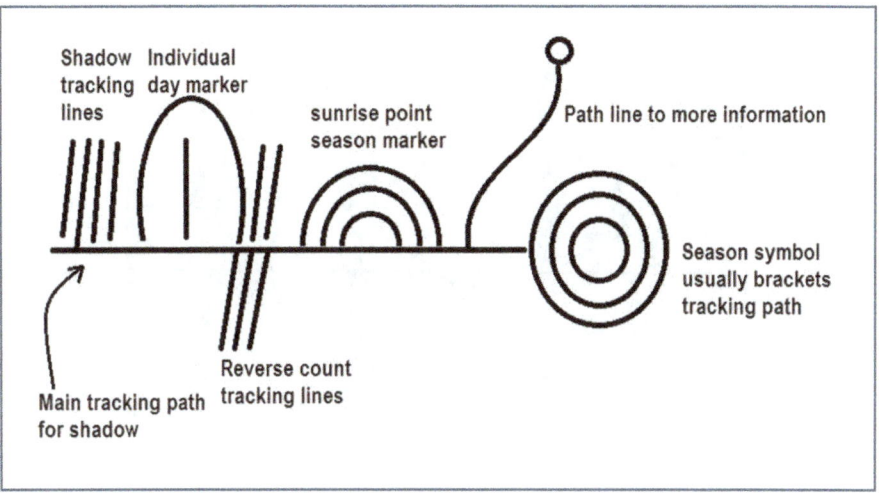

Photo 121 - A chart showing various shadow path symbols for daily tracking one will encounter.

Photo 122 - Panel in a wash that is a long and detailed daily tracking calendar along several sun shadow path lines. Note again the weather data above right.

Photo 123 - Panel at a remote spring tracking a long run of days

Photo 124 - A detailed rock panel that uses every crack to exacting usage for shadow lines from a rock top that casts a shadow from over 20 feet away and 20 ft higher. The rock panel appears to be moved into position so the shadow casts correctly and was even tilted somewhat. Note the season symbols bracketing each area.

Photo 125 - A great representative panel that uses a natural crack as the shadow line. Usually the crack would be carved to highlight it so it may just be a minor tracking line compared to others. Any rock incorporation should be considered before excluding.

Photo 126 - Notice the shadows point protruding and just missing the season symbol? This means the recorded date is not upon the site yet. But looking closely, you can see the tip of the shadow matches the shadow line under the circle exactly when it does line up.

Vertical Shadow Paths

Depending on the rocks shape the sun path may go upward or sideways. Notice on Photo 127 the shadow "notch" residing on the general sun symbol here where the radiating lines actually match the shadow angle (A). This general sun symbol (B) combination incorporating shadow lines (A) around it defies the minimum cutoff of using more than one circle to signify the sun. As it does not define a month, a season or specific event it is just a pointer used to mark the shadow path. Thus the context of the panel must be understood to properly interpret the symbol meaning. A shadow path is usually present to assist in your decision but the best indicators are the shadow path

Photo 127 - Shadow path and line on a vertical surface

radiating lines (A) and their slight mis-alignment with each other as "indicators" that they were used to match a shadows edge. Note the vertical path sun tracking line (C), the offset angles (D) each representing a progression in the yearly time marked when the sun shadow is cast upon that area of the path (C). Each of these steps has beside it a bit of data (E) drawn showing what happens during that time of the year. Water overflow of the lake bed, draining down the canyon, is one event during snow melt in spring, but the full purpose has not been studied.

Symbol Design Modified for Natural Shadow Shapes

Photo 128 is another cast shadow tip (A) just missing the left ring the Season symbol (B), but the shadow extension that has a dip (D) is centered under the vulva form (sun day symbol) (C). Just to the right exists a zig zag (E) form that matches exactly with the arrow tip of the shadow (F) to further track progression of the shadow trend as it moves along. Look closely at the correlation of the left tip (A) of the shadows inward curvature which matches the season symbols outer circle size. These slight adjustments on the symbols on the rock in all these symbols is a direct modification to adjust them to fit the shadow lines exactly. You will have to realize these modification reasons, sometimes without the shadows cast for comparisons, but once you see why they did it the reason such changes are present is obvious.

Photo 128 - Cast shadow

Multiple Site Time Segmentation

From the same Hickison Summit site in Nevada, Photos 129-130. The side panel is fully lit by the sun and you can clearly see the vertical and horizontal shadow path lines showing the division of information relevant for different times of the year. This is used to show multiple site occupation uses.

Photo 129 - Hickison, NV, side panel

Photo 130 - Hickison sun shadow

I could fill the book with tracked shadows like Photo 131, the point is to show the use without a doubt. These sites are used for tracking the year for many reasons. The sun location applications assist in this task instead of going to every site on every event each year. These tracking areas help define the reason for these

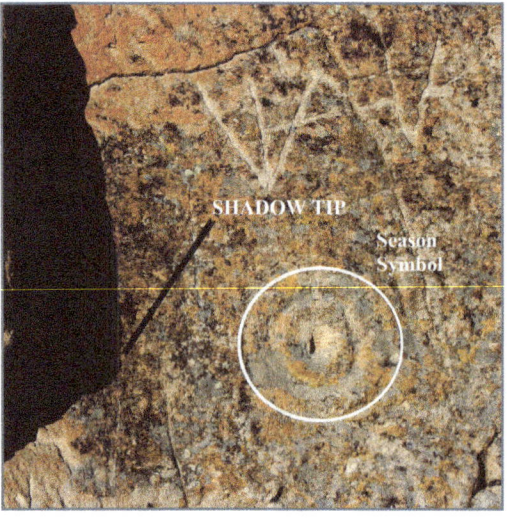

Photo 131 - Shadow tip approaching concentric circle season symbol

[Source: Author]

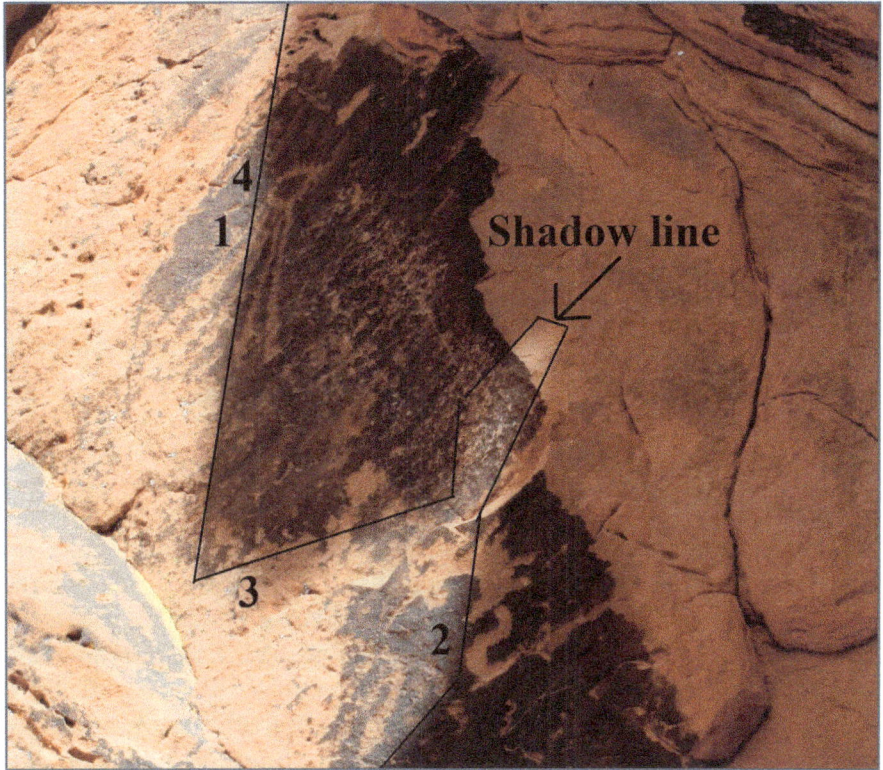

Photo 132 - Cast shadow

sites. This also shows an occupation site is near for such long term tracking to happen regularly.

As seen at Valley of Fire panel in Photo 132 the natural and man assisted wear of the surface coloring (3) yields a striking and visible shadow path edging, using contrast, that matches the actual shadow shown outlined. #4 sun symbol #4 has the radiating shadow lines (1) which appear tattooed (see tattooing) across the darkened area to designate it, but in actuality the radiating lines are defined and sharp and do end at shadow paths and thus tattooing was not the use here, it was actual lines to designate several shadow locations. Again as seen in (2) quadruped symbol is placed on this extension of shadow to designate time the travel took place. Any motion or animation took time and that time is one of the key data pieces to include if a story is to be told. The most used form of showing a time is a shadow casting on a symbol in Universal Language and so is heavily used in the quadruped interpretation. Quadruped usage I first discovered after breaking the season count panels because the direction matched the head direction of the animal and bracketed the quadruped symbols.

Squares of Land

Upon the ground today exists everyone's yards, fenced and neatly surrounding a square house with square windows and doors. Somewhat unnatural in design the square rules our lives. It did then as well and the square symbol is simply the designation of a person or groups land or plot.

In Photo 133, the plot is owned by a group or someone who is alive and who upkeeps the land within it. There is one exception—the graveyard plot. It is a square owned by a family, but nobody has to be living for it to remain in their possession. The land will be crop plots, harvesting plots, hunting rights, occupation locations, ship landings at port, gliding paths, and other things dealing with and on a physical piece of land.

Photo 133 - Land ownership squares

Here is a same-site difference at Lagamarsino site on Photo 134 showing a panel just down the ridge from a burial site plot of the growing site in a volcanic rock field and a plot group of crop growing area ownership located below the the cliffs.

Photo 134 - Growing site for food [Source: Author]

Photo 135 - Great example of rounded land lines and confusing data. The panel was further used as a grinding stone for pinyon pine nuts and destroyed data visibility.

Photo 136 depicts another unique land ownership group high in the mountains. The rock incorporation path along the entire top edge of the rock designates the drop off from this plateau to the valley area and a heavy animal trail and links the story as a divided story connected to the season symbols used as Brackets for this story (see Bracketing). The heavy pecked dots, I will say again, are not a "type" of drawing, but simply the large sap bearing trees represented that were here before they were cut down and turned into charcoal like all of the ancient trees around the state. Sap was crucial to the ships used in the lakes. Only the pinyon pine forests mostly survive now but back then there were the first groves of pinyon pines planted for cultivating the nut meal and thus spread throughout the west. The two winter symbols are present above showing the land ownership is claimed during these times close to the spring here as central brackets of the story.

Photo 136 - A land ownership panel depicting tree growths.

Gravesite Squares

The photo below (Photo 137) is from the Author's collection of main graveyard panel artistically denoting a snake head classically using the season symbol brackets as the eyes.

Photo 137 - Land plot of the graveyard keeping with the snake theme

The image shown in Photo 138 is from a Nevada occupation site with a graveyard along the direct route to the creek below the camp. The steep hillside is dangerous in the rocks around this graveyard so a path was made with great labor around the graves to the camp above. Walking along the path the headstones are present and this amazing artistic graveyard keystone panel that looks like a snake head! Behind this panel of the head rests the other panel shown of a snakes scaly body, again artistically represented, but is actually the simple square symbols of land graveyard ownership. This region was used in the winter and contains a massive rattlesnake den where snakes were harvested, represented in the theme snake images shown. The deaths due to this work may be mostly related to the snakes.

Photo 138 - Land plot of the graveyard keeping with the snake theme

ANCIENT UNIVERSAL LANGUAGE OF MAN

Squares for Sun Tracking

This image (Photo 139) is a notation using shadow lines for sun path tracking of the first of the winter solstice and vertical count lines make squares which are not representing land.

Photo 139 - Square symbol similarity from vertical day tracking lines drawn in line.

Photo 140 - Very similar to previous photo

Photo 140 is a creek side harvesting site. This map is on the reverse side of one keystone rock. The season symbols are shown above and below the shadow path line and the top season symbol is attached to the squares, which are also beside the shadow path line. Notice closely the vertical lines comprising the squares are not fully connected on both ends to horizontal shadow lines. The combined symbols associated with these squares make the squares a counting chart associated with the seasons and sun, so it is NOT a land ownership symbol. You must use the associated symbols to determine if they are land ownership squares or solar tracking lines as it is used about 50 percent of the time in either use, because shadow lines and vertical tracking lines simply make a square shape and so depicts solar events (and sometimes one day or night per square) easily. Remember land ownership, like today, can be patterns of connected shapes differing from each other, sometimes looking like doodles. So combinations of straight lines and rounded lines can also mean land.

Month Symbols

For years after I cracked the season symbols I decided it was enough for ancient peoples to simply know the changing weather to the degree of the seasons only. Again I was thinking like scholars and ignoring what I knew that ancients were highly intelligent and smarter than that. I started to attack the presence of other symbols and time marks on season symbols to see how simple ways could be used to track more delineations of the seasons. What happened after was a progression of realizations that lead to a fascinating discovery—they used month symbols! All the modern knowledge written had many types of months for the year and numbers of months. Following a simple lunar cycle you count thirteen months a year, but the ancients were smart and used twelve months just like we do. Note other civilizations used thirteen months, twenty six months and so many other configurations there could be additions to this original Universal Language symbology for a particular region, even in the same region overlapping an older society. Again, learning Universal Language allows adaptations but also allows decipherment of those changes.

Counting every symbol, included in the Universal Language combined, I will never crack a more complex symbol group. I can understand how these symbols have eluded every human since the knowledge was lost. I now present the most amazing written connection to nature and the most beautiful of the ancient Universal Language symbology.

Continuous Paths

I started understanding the month concept early on, but it mimicked the Season symbols so close that I decided they were segments of a season using two spiral forms, left and right twisting spirals. In the core sense a spiral is a continuous path symbol and can mean to turn over if a single looping spiral is attached to something such as a dead body. A short loop spiral mimicked by sign language movement can denote rotation, which in turn includes the concept "beginning" and "ending" (the start of the loop designates beginning and the end of the loop the ending). So as a core meaning the spiral represents a cycle and can expand from a core to a fixed meaning by using more spirals designating a fixed set symbol group. Thus having a dawning and setting like a solar day has, a lunar cycle, or the movement through a month. Finally this progression of realization allowed me to compare it to solar movements and science to unlock one of the most enigmatic symbols to see it was a monthly tracking symbol. The breakthrough took visiting hundreds of sites throughout the west coast before I made the mighty connection I am most proud of. That each of the spiral symbols denotes a separate month on the natural yearly calendar of the sun. What is this natural calendar I refer to? Read on.

Spirals

Photo 141 shows the serpent step edge down the pyramid casts a shadow on the spring and autumnal equinox sunrise and sunset.

Photo 141 - Photo from sun serpent head of the Temple of Kukulcan, showing a spiral. Photo by Vicki Andersen, Freelance Journalist.

Photo 142 - From Author's collection of Signal Hill, Arizona, of the top spiral symbol on the hill used to track the winter solstice designated as the month of December.

Analemma Into Spirals

Photo 143 is the Author's photo modified to show the weekly points in the sky throughout the year of the sun if you were to take them at the same time of day each time. You can see the figure 8 path it takes. The lowest point in the sky near horizon is winter solstice, the highest summer solstice. You can clearly see where the sun crosses its own path twice during crossovers to make the figure eight.

Photo 143 - Authors photo and drawing representing how the sun moves through the sky over the course of an entire year.

The combined diagram in Photo 144 first lists the Cassiopeia star system in tracking combination with the season symbol group in the left hand column. The second column represents the sun path through the sky at right, known as the Analemma, which makes a figure eight shown in above photo. Visible is the actual sun path, now seen to the left side in reverse using a shadow stick to cast shadows of the sun movement. This shadow reversal would also be flipped upside down from top to bottom due to shadow movement, however I left it facing the same way for easy reference of the included season symbols incorporated in the proper locations around the shadow and sun figures, so you can clearly see they are reversed as well. The third section depicts how you would display this figure eight analemma path in the form of a continuous spiral to show the monthly season symbol groups representing the full year in shadow spiral form.

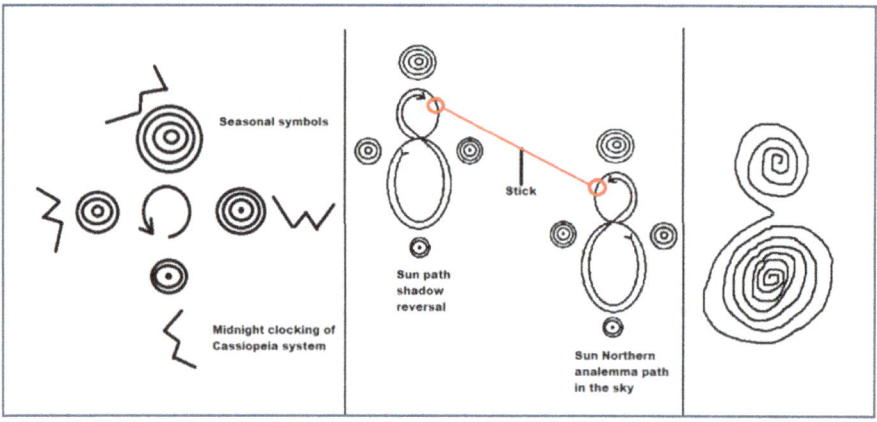

Photo 144 - Analemma direction and Cassiopeia association.

The analemma is the natural path the sun takes in the sky through the year and was used as the monthly calendar in ancient times. It is a figure eight the sun tracks in the sky and is made of a larger elliptical form due to the slower moving sun track in the sky that is a greater distance from the Earth through the Northern Hemisphere's colder months. And the smaller elliptic is due to the time the sun moves faster when the Earth is closest to the sun. Both due to the angle the sun hits as the tilt of the Earth changes this angle slightly as we circle the sun all year long. The sun shadow cast on a surface, if marked at the same time every day of the year, moves in this pattern and thus can be a tracking instrument for the month, season, and year.

Photo 145 shows how the sun moves along the horizon as it sets through the year. If the paths of direction going each way (north and south) from the

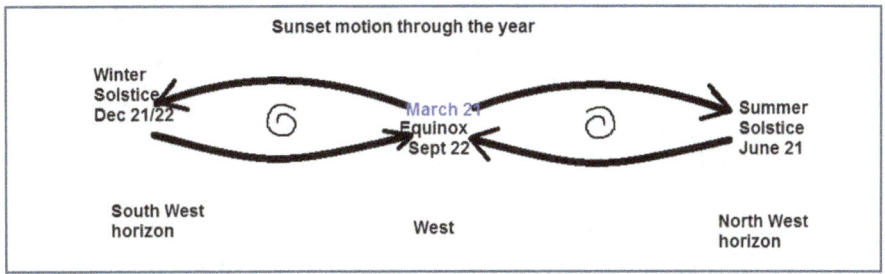

Photo 145 - Sunset motion through the year

centered equinox event, equalized by using arrows pointing away from each other and toward each other in a similar crossover harmony of the yearly cycle you also generate opposing spiral movements as shown.

SHADOWS

Since it is hard to grab a visual reference staring at the sun in an empty sky, the ideal way to track this natural movement is by casting a shadow on the ground to mark the location daily. The shadow on the ground when using a shadow stick casts a reverse shadow direction, so what is seen in the sky is reversed on the ground. Place that shadow path on a wall and you have a very apparent upside down version, in reverse. The very bottom of the path (the larger of the ovals) is Summer Solstice, at the top of the path (the larger oval) is Winter Solstice. The center culmination of the sun path completing the figure eight is called the crossover and happens twice a year as the sun first crosses in spring, and then crosses back over before Autumn. Midway on both sides of the larger oval of the elliptic path exist the Equinoxes. Of equal distances between the seasonal start dates exist the quarters, or halfway points between seasons and equinoxes and solstices. Along with these precessional events exist the major and minor movements of the sun and moon, and crossovers of the sun and moon each year. These advanced decipherments all have specific symbol markings that are not covered.

DIRECTION OF SPIRAL

The amazing thing with how man tracked time was to use this anelemma path. The clever thing was the fact they split the year and thus the months into the two DIRECTIONS OF ROTATION the sun path takes, not into a standard continual precessional count. So all of the months within each rotational direction starts the count (a spiral loop) from the first month in the loop and continues around, increasing with each month until the final month in the spiral. To simplify, they drew the spiral counts starting at the first of the

Year (all counterclockwise) and continued through the entire 7 months present in the counterclockwise (CCW) oval movement of the sun shadow path:

- January (1 CCW spiral)
- February (2 CCW spirals)
- March (3 CCW spirals),
- April (4 CCW spirals with an enclosed central spiral as a Dot to designate "first" and 4 CW spirals combined) **April 15th is the first Crossover of the Analemma and so the spirals switch from CCW to clockwise (CW) to represent the remainder of the month going into the other spiral, explained later.
- September (4 CCW spirals but with no center enclosed spiral like April has because this is the second crossover)
- October (5 CCW spirals)
- November (6 CCW spirals)
- December (7 CCW spirals)
- As you can see, there are 7 total CCW spirals, whereas there are only 5 CW spirals designating the five months of the smaller oval of the analemma
- May (1 CW spiral)
- June (2 CW spirals)
- July (3 CW spirals)
- August (4 CW spirals)

Remember we start at the very bottom of diagram on Photo 146 (January) and move toward the right directly into January. Directions of spirals simplified here for each month around the analemma circuit. Recall the bottom "oval" is where the sun shadow tracks around in a "Counter Clockwise" direction, hence all the month spirals around this are also represented as counterclockwise. The top "oval" sun tracks in a reverse direction to track Clockwise and so all five months spiral clockwise as well. Only April crosses into both oval areas, thus that month takes on a S shaped double spiral, the lower going CCW the upper going CW.

Photo 146 - Simplified spiral direction in associated time frame of analemma.

ANCIENT UNIVERSAL LANGUAGE OF MAN

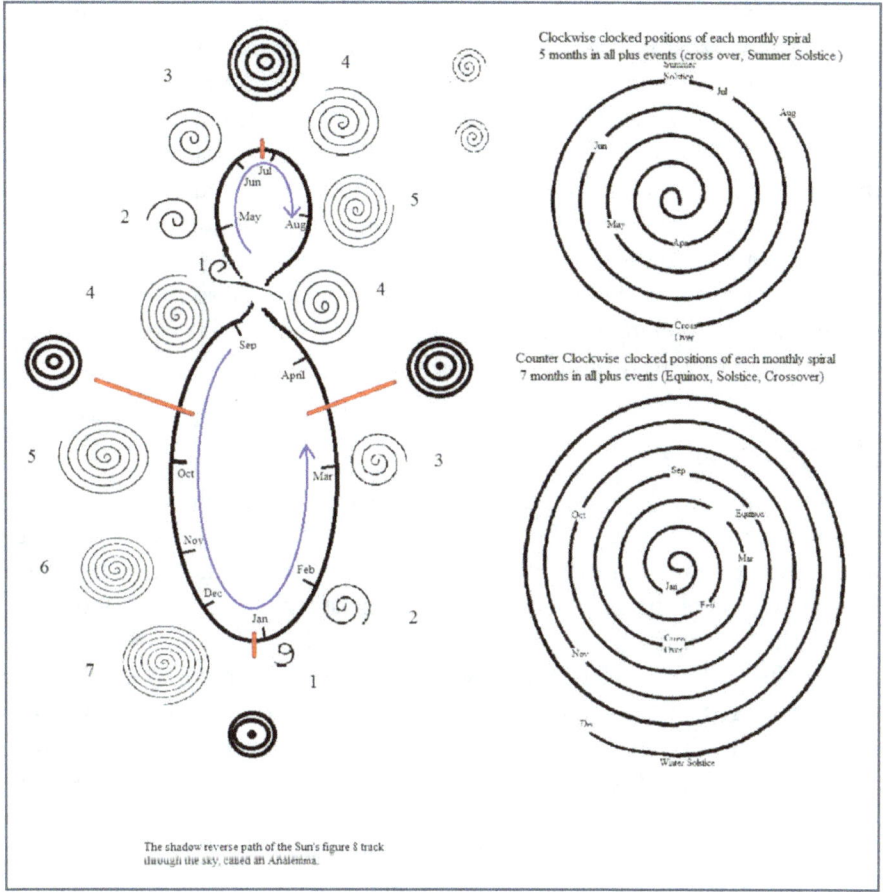

Photo 147 - Spiral reference to sun position in a shadow.

In Photo 147, the months are listed to the inside of the path line of the analemma, each counting January as 1 and counting consecutively upward as indicated by the blue arrow and jump from April to September to continue the counterclockwise direction until December (number 7) is reached. In the top half of the figure eight spiral exists the remaining five months from May and ending August.

To the right of this diagram are two large spirals representing the full monthly counts of each direction in a combined format. To start each spiral month you start from the outermost line of any spiral and count moving inward. This is how the spirals are meant to be read and conforms to sign language with the finger mimicking a spiral movement going inward. This conforms to following the outer circumference when drawing off the analemma oval shape of marked shadow paths on rocks.

The proper position around the outside surface of the drawn spiral depends on the start of the month on the full analemma path. So January 1 would position the start of the spiral line at dead bottom (because on the analemma shadow path the start of the year is dead bottom, or six o'clock on a clock face). February spiral would then start slightly clocked to the right (five o'clock position) and so on, clocking slightly more counterclockwise as you position the starting point of each month around the analemma shadow path. The month names are listed at the proper clocked starting positions within each spiral to show this. Since January is a single spiral, the very inside of the spiral belongs to January. As you move outward (from center each time) you find the next month and so on.

Crossover

As mentioned the analemma path crosses itself twice during its journey through the sky each year. The first crossover is after spring equinox and before summer equinox, in the middle of April and so the month shares both oval directions of the sun. Upon return of the sun at the end of August and just in the beginning of September it crosses back over for the second time (being after summer solstice and before autumnal equinox). This return to the central crossover point also makes it a third and central centering of the sun. All of these magical combinations make for a crazy human interest in it and probably one of the biggest celebrated moments every year. Hence all of the amazing symbol combinations out there in the world denoting it.

There are a variety of differences possible in the world for this situation marking the months surrounding this event. I am unsure the wording used as the names of each month back then but the fact appears to present a divided month that is started and then "paused" upon crossing over the first time and then "restarted" once the second crossover happens. In other words, April appears to share similar numbering with September on the spiral circuit! The spiral count is identical except April's four spirals has a solid dot in the center (or full circle) denoting "first" and September does not. This means they considered it a month that paused halfway through and then started again to completion once the crossover happened again. April ends the counterclockwise at four spirals, but upon the first crossover, starts the clockwise spiral count of one. Then after crossing back over starts September (still thought of as April) in the fourth CCW spiral count until the month of October starts at the fifth spiral. Being April and September are between the crossover and both Equinoxes also makes for a unique monthly connection of equality.

Author's image on Photo 148 showing a crossover grouping. Right is a spiral with CCW 5 (August) with a center that is a fully enclosed circle (hitting Crossover). Left is CW three spiral with centered tail and semi-enclosed center showing "partial," meaning this tracking went into June and slightly into the month of July. So close to the start of summer through August is the timeframe covered at this site.

Many sites have similar configurations like Photo 149. Remember the long tails go up to a point exactly targeted as the shadow location that was marked for the given month. Sometimes the center of the spiral is marked if a site is perfect for shadow casting on a surface that made that designer choose how his format would be written.

Photo 150 shows separated month symbols of April and September to show the harmony on

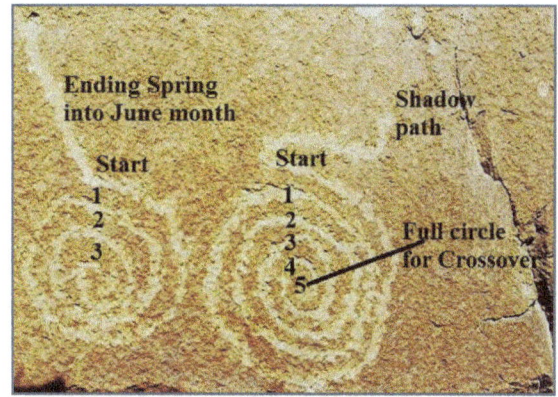

Photo 148 - Crossover group

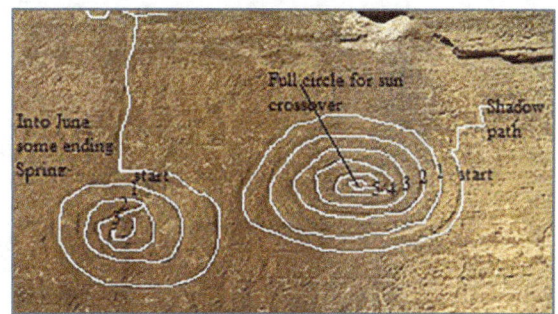

Photo 149 - Another crossover panel

both sides of the lower oval of the crossover and between both equinoxes.

In Author's Photo 150, the image shows the crossover (A), where April opposing "S" spirals are drawn in raw format showing spiral in correct shadow path format upside down. This type of configuration is referenced this way in several examples and to connect the top of the analemma CW spiral

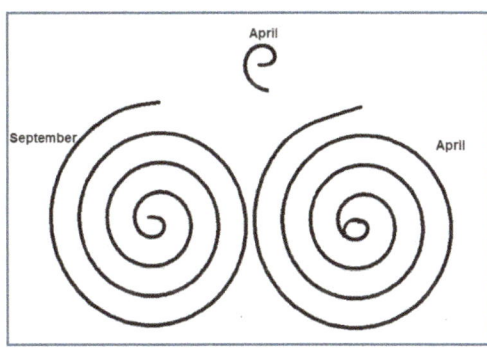

Photo 150 - Before and after crossovers drawing by Author. Note a fully enclosed center circle on the right in the spiral shows "first" crossover "A point" (in time) and "sooner."

Photo 151

properly (the lower smaller spiral of A) it is connected to the end of the bigger CCW spiral in a projected shadow configuration (a shadow casts reverse as described earlier, thus a high sun in the sky will cast a shadow lower on the rock and vice versa). Captured Summer solstice (B) and captured Autumnal equinox (C). Note pinched index finger and thumb at left side of Autumn (C) symbol just beside the connected vertical shadow path line that is integrated in the spiral.

Photo 152 - Author's photo of a panel showing from left day count bar (3D), Spring symbol, Crossover solid dot enclosed in circle and small spiral (start of April count after crossover).

Photo 153 - Photo of Newgrange famous triple spirals modified by Author to show combination of separate spirals interacting.

Photo 154 - Author's photo of a 3D crossover designation (left) beside a 1D August symbol (right).

Photo 155 - Author's photo of a main tracking panel at a site dedicated to tracking the entire year. Note hand around spiral and zigzags coming down as count lines.

In Photo 155 the panel captures Summer Solstice (C). Top (A) is continued tracking of the Autumn season. Top right (B) is the classic zigzag count paths going down beside the natural crack to the main symbol, the 3 CW spiral with a dead calf cut center circle denoting June 22-23. (C) captured into the form of the closed hand. The top of the spiral shows the index finger (D) and shows the hand is a intricate part of this symbol creation.

Equality of Season Month

Author's Photo 156 of a referencing panel showing the equality (the curved = equal sign of the human arms and legs between the symbols) showing the correlation of the New Year monthly symbol for January and the Winter Solstice symbol.

Photo 156 -Month and winter correlation panel [Source: Author]

Circumference Data of Months

As with the Season and Moon Symbol groups, there are plenty of circumference examples with the Month spiral group like in Photo 157 for the obvious reason that circumference data can be placed on any symbol for displaying more data. The story through the month's days can be told in great detail and in order following the spiral direction starting from the beginning of the spiral around.

Photo 157 - Showing August extra data around the perimeter

CHRIS HEGG

2D AND 3D REPRESENTATION OF THE SYMBOLS

Shown in Photo 158 is a wonderful example of someone who created the panel with forethought in mind by representing TWO styles together in a way the single shadow casts across both styles in proper order. This could well be the origin location for the creation of the newer style 3D symbols! This is an amazing piece and I thank Logan so much for allowing me to show these pictures to the world. At the left side shows the older 2D style of the yearly tracking symbols in the form of actual finger depictions of sign language circling the quadruped symbol showing the movement direction. I included the finger symbol in rotational context next to each of the symbols. To the right is the newer 3D more square artistic spiral symbol in direct

Photo 158 - Photo modified from original taken by Logan Ray Bier from a hilltop

relation to the finger as proof. The square 3D symbology is listed in lines instead of circular, which allows many easier ways to use the original symbols in a linear layout much like written language now. Such as seen around pottery, rugs and baskets and other decorations people thought were just pure decoration.

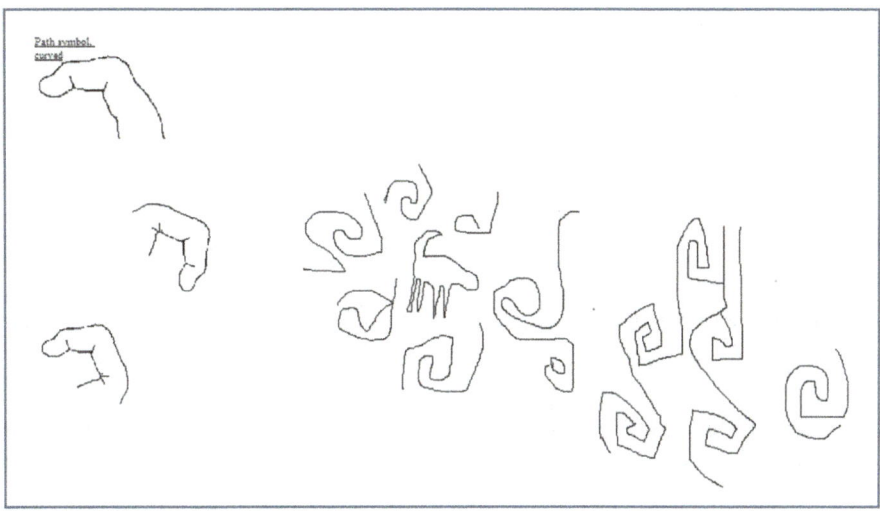

Photo 159 - Author's drawing of the panel for clarity

Photo 160 and 161 is another panel by Logan Ray Bier of the original 1D spiral style found on the same rock outcrop. The creator made all three styles in the same place just for reference where room allowed.

Photo 160 - Photo by Logan Ray Bier of side panel

Photo 161 - Photo by Logan Ray Bier showing front panel

Megalithic Usage

Like the incorporation of the season symbols into megalithic relics of the past, there are hundreds of massive sites that incorporate the month symbol groups.

Painting of aerial view of Knowth Site, obvious now as an analemma with the month symbols located properly along the figure 8 main form but now covered enough not to be able to see more than a group of hills. Represented in the megalithic site is the full analemma figure eight form represented in the two bigger mounds and the "13" months each of the smaller mounds surrounding the sun path shape.

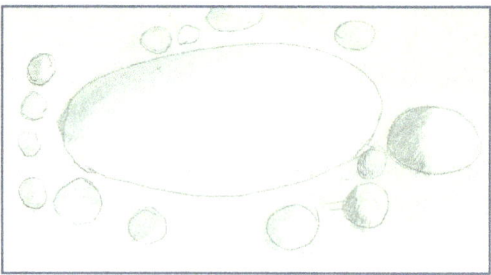

Photo 162 - Painting by Willow Phillips of Knowth Site

Photo 163 - Tail spiral of the "Serpent Mound" United States. Again the beginning of the new year month. [Source: Author]

Photo 164 Nasca Lines, Peru, drawing by Author showing reference to the crossover month.

To demonstrate an entire vast region of hundreds of miles of valleys of intaglios carved into the playas of the tracking of months by symbols, visit images of Verneukpan, South Africa, to see the extent and sites of ancient cities around them. Surprisingly not heard of by most but far larger and more complex compared to the Nasca Lines.

Photo 165 by Author of the Phaistos Disk, a undecy-

Photo 164 - Drawing source: Author, Nasca Lines monkey geoglyph showing tail as a month symbol as many new symbols do that have just been discovered when the winds blew sand away exposing them.

pherable object thought to be from Troy. I believe it is used as a double sided stamp created in reverse to portray a proper directional stamped image of the entire monthly cycle of the year using the shadow spiral analemma symbology with sectioning lines denoting times of the year. The outer marks denote the months and the crossover path can be seen in the 90 degree lines contacting the edge, creating the path of the April month extension from one part of the analemma lower elliptic area to the top elliptic.

Photo 165 - The Phaistos Disk is thought to be a board game or many other things. It is a printing press for the year represented in the correct spiral direction and month numbers per each of the clockwise and counter clockwise directions of each month spiral in shadow cast form (reversed). [Source: Approved use by © 2001 Bruce Blankinship

Micro Decipherment Secrets

I want to share with you a very interesting type of decipherment that I have implemented. It is both a technique and method used in many panels and outlines the details, sometimes in plain sight, yet in secrecy if you are not familiar with the process. If you fail to look at the smallest of tiny details in the panel pecking you will possibly miss the main explanation. The micro mechanics of the drawing is direct evidence of such intense focus by the creator of the panel that you should pay close attention to these details while you are present and take close photographs of these details. Large full encompassing images of the panel will miss these fine renditions of simple things like paths, footsteps, body angles. And even some parts of the day could shadow or sun over the areas leaving you thinking nothing small exists. Several visits may be necessary to get everything you did not see the first time around.

Photo 166 is an image of two common symbol groups combined. It is an initial thought that this is a spring of water an animal is drinking at because it just looks that way. Nothing appears out of character compared to any glyph symbols you seen before probably. Now lets compare it to a known object in Photo 167.

Photo 166 - Apparent normal symbol drawn [Source: Author]

The fact the entire panel is this tiny is unique. Below and horizontal in the image is a human symbol with the quadruped above and then the winter season symbol pack. A lot of tiny intricate detail to say an animal drinks at a spring like I once thought it meant when I was 12 years old. Why would anything of this nature be written so tiny when vast amounts of room exists to draw on?

Photo 167 - Actual tiny size of panel shown with a quarter as reference

Photo 168 is another example panel. It is designating a route to a hidden cave group (1) on top of a mountain side (6) using rock incorporation for the cave mouth using existing vesicles in the rock and the outline of the mountain range in general is seen by the differences of texture and shapes natural on the rock above and below the whitened contact line, mimicking the ACTUAL mountain tops. The journey up can be seen in the three individuals packing supplies on their backs up the trail. (2) figure shows turned toward the cave and neck elongated to show path direction clearer. (3) figure shows the wide body of a pack on him. (4) figure is larger to show closer to the panel on the journey and is used to

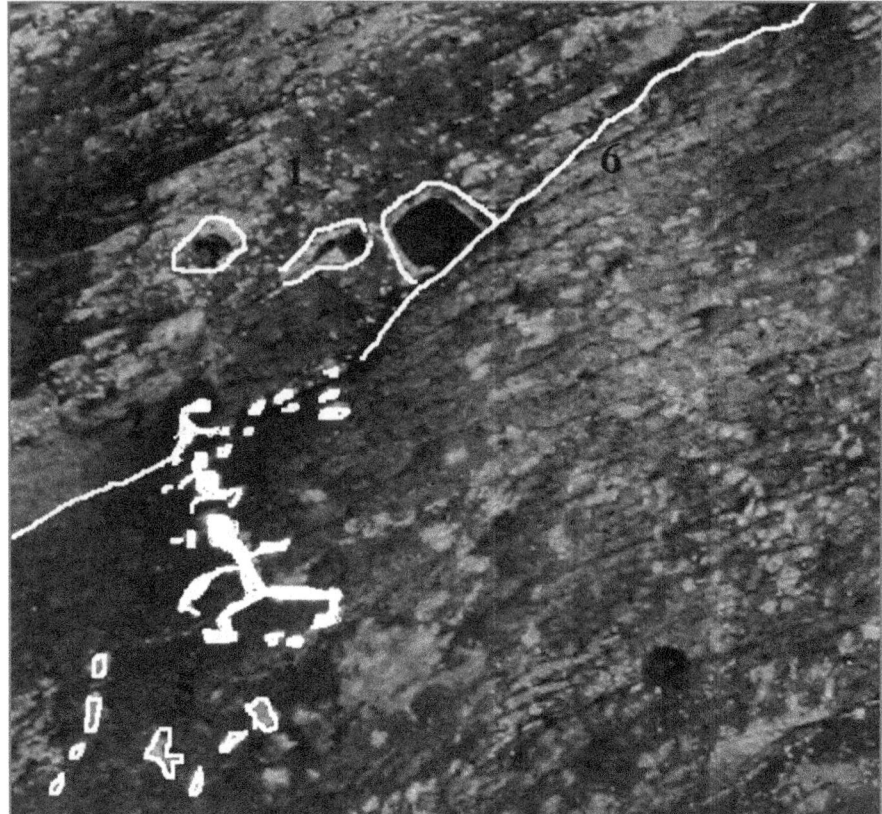

Photo 168 - A micro panel attached to a bigger panel [Source: Author]

show the movements of climbing up a path. (5) foot print symbols show the various paths up the mountain used and that they left prints. A quadruped form could be used here, but this information is very secret and very much about the group that uses the cave and not the journeys that took place up the mountain. In other words, secret information to the hidden cave, hidden in plain sight. They wanted to tell the story of the path, cave and mountain used here, but still keep it under wraps if you were not familiar with the language.

Note this hard rock does not accept pecking well and again looking at every tick mark the creator attempted helps you understand what he was trying to share with you the reader. The pecks may not produce a rich picture at this depth, but you can see the path of footprints stagger left to right to show footprints and the sizing to the human forms match and the curve of the path shows going up to the caves at an angle. In this case up a wash.

Photo 169 is the full panel of Photo 168 zoomed out, the area seen in Photo 169 covers only a 3" x 3" square of this panel—so small it was impossible to

Photo 169 - Tiny panel in referenced location of the full panel. Now note the correlation to the actual mountain range terrain seen above it [Source: Author]

get any better pecking drawing on the spot. But now seen here in relation to the mountain range miles from the panel, you can now appreciate just how amazing the rock texture and contours match that range so far away in small scale.

Tattooing Practice

Photo 169 is the best show of Tattooing I can present with the "mountain range" symbol drawn only across the rock face that naturally is shaped like the mountain range so it is clear to the reader you are to observe the rock incorporation MAINLY to understand the secret being told. Notice how the tattooed image flows across the rock portion intended in a wide swath somewhat off angle and not super defined, but clearly stretching the symbol line to the top contact with the mountain range top and clear to the bottom in the ravine represented in the large open crack of the rock. This generalized depiction also attempts to convey it is meant as a tattoo to accent what nature already provided for the story to be told on this rock.

GRAVEYARD SYMBOLS

It is interesting to think of our desire to mourn death in two opposite ways. First, we start the process with a soft, bright colored delicate flower. The flower remains bright and then fades quickly after. We like to follow religious beliefs in burial process that takes some time for preparation, even cremation, prior to public display of flowers. Then in most instances, the permanence of the situation of passing must be dealt with so the dead is memorialized by their information being marked onto stone and metal, a surface to survive the trials of eternity. Our humanity has always remained human and a loss is hard as well. One thing is clear, no one wants to die alone or be dead forever—alone. Every religion suggests grouping after death, maybe indicating our worst fear and feeling to life is the singular corporeal existence we live here will be over when we pass. Even corpses must be placed together when buried, closer together if you're family. A remote elder dying alone may be found and simply stuffed in a small crack out of respect, having nobody who loved him or who got lost, but in groups everyone has someone and I think everyone desires someone who will be there for you when you pass.

FLOWERS

Photo 170 represents the symbol of Universal Language that remains in the human psyche to this day depicts specifically the graveyard and the

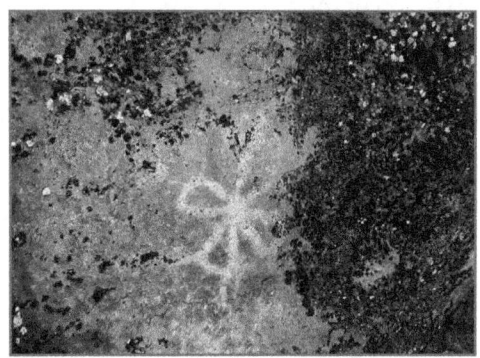

Photo 170 - A graveyard designator flower symbol [Source: Author]

Photo 171 - Graveyard indicator along route. Note the flowers going up with the stems from bottom side to on top of rock [Source: Author]

association of death—the flower! The actual depiction of large flowers are used to designate a grave area, usually of a larger nature. The path along the route to the graveyard is covered in flowers as well. Some flower styles, like bells are depicted in harvesting sites, for the blue color used for dyes or edible types. A larger open type petal flower is usually reserved for graves and not just any flower like in Photo 171.

Note in Photo 171 the larger flower on the second photo with stem going up to top of rock.

Flower symbols are seen directly at the site prior to entering the graveyard and the flower designates the site as a Holy place. The fact that the flower is used for death then and now shows a natural need of man to incorporate beauty into the sad fact of death. Maybe the renewal of life after death? Many sites with graves have unnatural amounts of flower bloom as well, leading to the possibility that flowers were seeded in these spots to bloom yearly. Research indicates flowers mask the smell of decay and that may well be the first use in death.

Holy Site Warning Symbol

Another symbol for graveyards and other locations where death was heavy is seen prior to entering the restricted area is the human form with big hands extended and open in warning of a sacred site and to stay clear as seen in Photo 172-177.

Photo 172 - 177 - Author's conglomerate of Holly Site warning photos

In Photo 178 we see the human form with big hands and feet with open arm position is used exclusively for these sites, but in most instances the graveyards, if moderate sized, exist within the occupation areas and just like now, graveyards were placed near the housing zone so it could be visited regularly and the deceased can be kept close.

Photo 178 - Photo by Author of the Holly Site symbol panel

The Dead Honored

In many sites the graveyard is actually placed between the areas of camp and water or other paths that were used regularly to further assure visitation. Meaning they cared about the dead maybe more than us? Gravesites create much confusion into the world of Universal Language, because the person's name is listed, which has singular odd forms of symbols. Usually not so generalized and thus seeing these sites will make you think there are a thousand more symbols you don't know, but in fact is symbol combinations used for a name unique to that individual.

Photo 179 - Author's photo, I do not have unique symbol understanding for everything, but this "happy bald guy buried here" to sum up the description carved, deserves a place in this book.

Photo 180 - Photo by Author of representative compiled headstone group in a graveyard denoting the names of the dead buried below them.

Photo 181 - Author's photo showing just the lower of one section of a central graveyard, comprising of ten large flows of basalt covering a mountain.

CENTRAL GRAVEYARDS

This ancient empire cared for their dead more than we did. A perfect example for this is seen in the massive central empire graveyards (see Photo 181 as example). Placed in the middle of their inland lake territory there stretched a centralized chain of permanent graveyards where the dead were laid to rest and visited by the living. Generations of family were buried in the same spots. So understanding that these most defendable central regions were given up to house the reveals the level of commitment the ancient living had for their dead.

GRAVEYARD TYPES

I have broken graveyards into three types: Local, satellite and central. Local comprises of smaller settlement groupings of graves specific to the families existing there, even if it was occupied in shorter times of the year as groups migrated. Satellite graveyards exist where no occupation sites exist and were made as temporary hold over locations while the bodies were decomposing and left to natural elements before being transported to a central or local site. Temporary satellite sites sometimes only had one grave or a few and were later abandoned when the remains and the petroglyph rock were transported from the area to another spot. War areas sometimes makes satellite sites that remain permanent. I have found many satellite sites abandoned but obviously used. Graveyards (and why many say, "Where are all the ancients then?") are located exclusively in volcanic detritus piles along hillsides. The bodies bones are buried in deep pits dug round into the rock piles. Sometimes in layers as more family members are buried one above the other or beside another until the hole is filled up. The upper rocks are sometimes just the names of the last occupants in the pits or sometimes the rocks are moved up and put together to show all in the pit. Some name rocks are moved

Photo 182 - Author's photo of satellite graveyard used after a war. Occupation existed in this canyon as well.

as it is filled. The rounded pits are usually six- to seven-feet deep and up to six-feet wide like in Photo 183. The rocks are dug out and then a circular stacking is made inside to retain the pits structure from collapse like a well as the rock around it is layered back against the pit walls until just the pit remains. As it fills with deceased the pit depth shrinks and layers of rock are placed back in level high enough to cover the remains. The name rocks are placed around the pits walls usually facing east but really can be in many directions. Any side hill full of cobble rock can be a graveyard. Some central empire graveyards are massive and contain thousands of dead. The use of cremation was common and widely used. Some evidence found on mummified ancients like the Spirit Man uncovered in Churchill County, Nevada, show that several humans ashes were carried in pouches on a person, presumably family. Spirit Man himself was in a cave wrapped for burial by someone who loved him. This clearly shows ancients took care of their elder and that there was a place for them 9,500 years ago and beyond. Information at http://en.wikipedia.org/wiki/Spirit_Cave_mummy

Photo 183 - Author's photo, half open burial pit.

Below is author's photo of the "Eyes" rock centrally located in the cemetery, always watching the graveyard flows. This one volcanic flow of rocks I refer to as "flow one" goes almost a half mile long and over 600' wide. This particular graveyard is over 2 miles wide and 6 miles long. To date I have never found the ends of it. It is located in the center of the ancient empire that existed here and resides within a mountain range which was surrounded by great lakes on most sides 16,000 years ago.

Photo 184 - Most large graveyards exhibit one or more "Watchman" rock panels that represent a large rock giant almost for a final warning of watching over you while you are there [Source: Author]

Younger Petroglyphs

Spanish Miners

Photo 185 is a old native silver Spanish mine where an Indian observer sat above the mountain watching and documented this event. Written is the event of a worker (E) exiting the mine (A) (upside down U shaped path) with a upside down bat (B) hanging. Running on fire (C) with visible specks of ash and smoke coming off of his back as he moves forward toward the right. Notice the 3 fire symbol fingers (D) representing fire, in straight bird feet

Photo 185 - Spanish spied on by Indians [Source: Author]

pattern (fear) and his legs in moving form (F) the right foot bent and showing direction away from the mine. The fact he is drawn in fully and thick represents a "bad covering" of injury and fire. An apparent black powder ignition incident or the original method of pitch covering the rock then building a pile of wood on the mine face and burning it to heat the rock, then pouring water on the rock to crack it may have went wrong. There are attempts around the cliff to denote Spanish symbols to clarify who they watched. The man lay dead or unconscious (G) afterward. After is depicted in smaller form but inline with the story progression. Being drawn after the natural rock fracture this can also mean he was some distance before collapsing. The mine was mined yearly in early spring to fall and a pack mule (H) and another Spanish person (I) is also listed.

Defensive

Photo 186 is Author photo of White Mountain City ghost town, California, showing a very small portion of defensive rock works that extends layer after layer and includes outposts, and lookout posts due to Indians attacking the town.

White Mountain City was a white settlement made famous by Mark Twain and fascinating to visit. The site has thousands of feet of rock fortifications surrounding it due to constant Indian raids and they were not heard of for months when a rescue party was sent due to one major blockade by Indians. The panels seen on Photo 187 show detailed data of the zigzag fortifications including strong points and complete time data of the siege designated by the moon symbols shown and the supplies brought by the whites who broke the siege.

Photo 186 - Rock defensive walls built due to Indian raids at White Mountain City [Source: Author]

Photo 187 - Defensive position and offensive data recorded on whites activities inside the town [Source: Author]

WAGONS

Wagon wheels were a new introduction in North America along with whites and pack animals. In Photo 188, by Guy Starbuck, a wagon train en route is depicted. Note the animals pulling the wagon, the driver, the walking man with the gun and dog and the fact the designer used rock incorporation with the slight edging to help the drawing dimensions.

Photo 188 - Photo Wagon Train by Guy Starbuck ©, Http://Starbuck.org/exploring

Mammoths

Upon these lands 16,000 years ago were mammoths. They were used in the art of human warfare and supply packing.

Mammoth symbols provide an interesting and actual rendition to the animal worth mentioning in this book. It is interesting to watch historic recreated television documentaries on the mammoth and human interaction and NONE show a much more connected life of mammoths with humans as their trained animals. Obviously humans had ancient horses as pack animals, and mammoths used for riding and war. Mammoth hunting injuries are well documented and would still occur with raging animals injured by humans to kill even while riding a mammoth. Petroglyphs suggest mammoth herds managed by human groups existed in some areas. Mammoths trained young could easily provide much of the labor tasks and pack duties of the ancients and be transported by boat for war and other duties.

Photo 189 is a petroglyph at Grimes Point, Nevada, is the burial site of a great mammoth trainer

Photo 189 - Author's original photo of Mammoth seen as panel is today

Photo 190 - Authors photo manipulated to see better

Photo 191 - Same picture extracted to see details minus rider

and warrior. The petroglyph is shown unchanged in authors original photo of mammoth, then to show how important enhancing some panels are in decipherment. Photo 190 and 192 are two modified pictures of the original to bring out useable information.

The use of these larger animals was so normal for transporting trade goods and supplies that the actual mammoth petroglyph image is hardly used, just like many of the mundane things we today use and never list since it is common knowledge. It is however present as quadruped movement symbols which makes it hard to prove sites usage sometimes as the mundane always gets overlooked and only special events or needed data is ever drawn on rocks. The elephant footprints are shown in several panels through the territory, but again many animals were used for packing. Therefore to show a camel, mammoth, and more would be unnecessary for usable data to anyone. As most trade and living was ON the water, land use is limited in these times just like the wheeled cart would be very useless.

Photo 192 - Author's photo of mammoth in a mud trap with ancient horse in background, Carson City, Nevada State Museum.

A similar image was found in Moab of Mastodons and by colleagues of the Smithsonian Institution and University of Florida http://newsdesk.si.edu/releases/scientists-reveal-first-ice-age-art. Thought by them to be the oldest mammoth image in America, engraved on a mammoth bone found in the Florida bog area dates to at least 13,000 years ago up to 20,000 years old, when most large Pleistocene animals went extinct in the eastern United States.

HANDS

The most connected symbol group to us in the written Universal Language is the human hand. They have been a fascination to me for well over 30 years of my life yet I dismissed it as a rare enigma that was neat, but unimportant. Over the decades it become more of a standing obstacle to break that I just could not dismiss. I pondered how such a hard design to carve, that appears differently many times, is not important? But how could a hand of an individual be information beyond describing something of the person?

My breakthrough came after visiting sites where I witnessed the hand symbol far too often and finally realized there were different types of hand symbols. Some hands were exact anatomical reproductions, usually from sprayed paint over a hand and appear done fast and haphazardly wherever they were at when they had to list the symbol, others had a circular palm. I noted all circular palms were directly associated with solar symbols. Some solar symbols, like the month and season, were incorporated into the palm itself. Showing the round palmed hand was very important. In a single visitation to a panel having both hand and feet the entire enigma was finally solved. Work continues on anatomically correct version meaning. I believe it is the same but unproven due to so many variations of locations with no other indicators around it.

ANCIENT UNIVERSAL LANGUAGE OF MAN

Blocking

Photo 193 open hand in sign language of Universal Language is used to show the act of "blocking." In this case the outstretched hand, palm open with fingers extended and open, shows blocking the sun from the eyes. This natural hand motion is used to portray what blocks the sun in nature, a yearly event but something that is extremely difficult to predict.

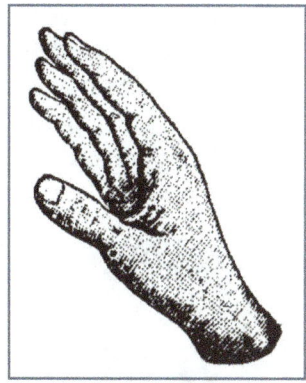

Solar Eclipses

Again, as seen in Photo 194 hand with the outstretched fingers is the sign for the Moon blocking the sun. The eclipse is very hard to predict on the move especially and as such was recorded in detail. Sometimes with paint sprayed over the hand as people and groups were traveling when it occurred. Eclipses can be minor to full and information was recorded and transferred so knowledge tracking them could be gained. The type of eclipse coverage

Photo 193 - Image from Sign Language Among North American Indians Compared With That Among Other Peoples and Deaf-Mutes First Annual Report of the Bureau of Ethnology to the 1881 (Garrick Mallery)

Photo 194 - Author's photo of the main portion of panel denoting the solar eclipse events.

was noted and any event data that was relevant. The hand has been noted in general panels as the moon symbol exclusively. Though the single circle with other symbols such as used in lunar counting exist, a hand appears to have taken the meaning of the moon. Eclipses were much more pronounced then and will disappear all together in the future as the moon moves away from the earth.

Photo 195 - Front and main season symbol keystone opposite the prior hand symbol photos that has been heavily vandalized on the upper symbol areas. Some of the symbols missing can be reconstructed knowing Universal Language.

ANCIENT UNIVERSAL LANGUAGE OF MAN

Photo 196 - Beyond bullet holes, the visibly round palm with fingers defining this type of symbol group in solar event count position one upon the other. [Source: Author]

Photo 197 - Sherri Bombard took this great shot of an eclipse sequence.

Photo 198 - Author's photo in Agua Fria National Monument again showing the circular palms with unrefined fingers radiating showing it is not meant for an eclipse and more of a meteor shower streaming debris. The rough designs make it hard to decide and shows a weakness of Universal Language.

Photo 199 - A great example of a round palm with fingers but the palm incorporates the winter solstice and season symbol directly with a 3D count cycle of squared bent fingers (witnessed earlier) from the date of solstice. [Source: Author]

Photo 200 - Photo taken by Willow Phillips showing probably the most famous petroglyph shown on T.V. documentaries said to display a supernova but is actually an eclipse. Note the unusual amount of fingers on the palm to the left.

CHRIS HEGG

THE FOOT

As the hand is the human symbol to show the moon above the user blocking the light of the sun, mimicking what the hand does. There is an opposite appendage and meaning for the reverse eclipse event witnessed in nature. The solar eclipse and the foot. The foot, opposite the hand, touches and walks upon the earth. Which in turn blocks the sun from the moon to create the solar eclipse. Used in signing sign language the foot is represented with bent shorter fingers to designate toes and a closed fist held under the open hand to designate the whole movement as a foot. Again the foot seems to have completely assimilated the use as describing the earth in all contexts.

These foot and hand opposites are unique and amazingly simple, yet defied anyone from cracking the code do to this simplicity. Just one more way the obvious and easy understanding of Universal Language can be remembered,

Photo 201 - Foot panel by Dennis Roshay

Photo 202 - Another foot symbol Photo and site discovery in Little Colorado River drainage by Dennis Rashay who has photographed many petroglyphs sites. Note the solar month and crossover symbols associated.

used and taught in the ancient's life. As with the palm being round to represent the moon's circular form and long fingers to represent the hand, the foot has the indignant form of being longer bodied with shorter toes to differentiate it yet keep it the similar recognized symbol group. The rounded heel designating the round earth instead of the moon. As with the lunar eclipse events, the solar eclipse also has various degrees of blocking the suns rays and thus varies in Universal Language drawing accordingly. Remember some foot symbols are not feet at all but pear cactus harvesting with blooming fruit on the tops, or loaded burden baskets. Both have a different shape and usually has separated toes from the main body, or the body shape is completely different. They may still be associated with any solar/season/monthly symbols for harvest times however.

Photo 203 - Photo by Win Heger, a petroglyph photographer. Foot symbol panel with month and a multi seasonal symbol group in Fredonia, Arizona.

Photo 204 - Photo by Carl Bjork photographing a horizontal foot in relation to his own.

ANCIENT UNIVERSAL LANGUAGE OF MAN

Petroglyph Location

Painting by Willow Phillips and Chris Hegg (digital Photo 205) visualizing the arrival at the floating city on south west Lahontan Lake, 16,000 years ago. Present day Walker Lake with Mt. Grant in the background. Valley Rivers that fed the floating city area with fresh water.

Photo 205 - Floating city of ancient Walker Lake drawn and painted by Willow Phillips and Chris Hegg.

Floating Cities

The ancients built massive cities that were regional. Because they not only sailed the seas—they lived on them. Most of the mighty ancient empire within the Great Basin lived on floating cities in the lakes. Harbored just off shore in calmer waters existed the docks and houses of many of the empires personnel. Only certain areas did they make continual shore living, which led to complete destruction of evidence of the actual size of the empire in America during that time. Another amazing accomplishment of an already amazing civilization. Petroglyph sites focus attention on these regional establishments and a future book will explain much of this topic.

Photo 206 - Grind stones sunk from cities once perched on the floating city pad [Source: Author]

Photo 206 from authors collection depicts numerous floating city process rocks such as these large grinding stones, lay strewn across the desert where they sunk after the floating city was abandoned and finally subsided due to no maintenance. Anchor points and anchors for these cities would also be present.

> http://www.archaeology.org/issues/145-1409/features/2367-peopling-the-americas-paradigms writes; *"If there's a new buzzword in the archaeological study of the peopling of the Americas, it is "boats." Part of reimagining the settling of the New World is to stop considering traveling by land as the only way people could have arrived there. "We so radically underestimated the roles of boats and water transports for all time horizons, not just the more recent past," Adovasio explains. After all, roughly 50,000 years ago aboriginal Australians completed the trip from East Africa to Oceania. More specifically, they got there via Asia, "and they sure didn't walk," says Collins. Evidence shows—and this is an important understanding to factor in when considering all of these migrations—that the "trip" took them 20,000 years.'* Mike Collins, Texas State University Archeologist

World Trade

The world was only flat in 1492. Before this for tens of thousands of years empires thrived and traded throughout the globe, which I attempt to prove in this book. Major petroglyph sites can be located within the Great Basin and many other parts of the world in remote and desolate locations. What you see are the locations now, not 13,000 years ago. Then the waters filled the basins. Causing natural ship passages through the interior of the mountain range "island chains" that lay within in the Great Basin en-echelon like snakes moving North in mass. These giant freshwater lakes were sources of massive food supplies and opened ice age snow and glacier covered regions by boat to pillage tradable goods.

As with all navigation we need aids. The petroglyph sites contained all the information of regional wind directions, freshwater, resources, local control personnel, weather statistics, time of year data for safety, and so on. The petroglyph locations were strategically placed at the furthest ends of each lake system and other landfall areas best suited to move supplies from one lake to another; or in supply gathering locations along the lake edges! These sites encompass docks and ports of natural and manmade design. Visible hills that can be seen while crossing the lakes and in inclement weather were panel sites. Spring water sources, campsites and boundary region markers between regional powers were also panel sites. Some sites are chosen for natural safe havens that are defendable and usable year round as midway points. Grimes Point Fallon, Nevada, exists several hidden caves and the land fingers out into the great lake, at times an island fortress.

Imagine yourself 20,000 years ago on the first expeditionary fleets roaming the American coasts finding inlets into these massive lakes. The reality you are with a smaller group so many months from home in an unexplored land full of giant animals and threats would weigh heavy on you. Ice sheets shedding into the lakes and adverse weather all able to kill you instantly with a sneeze. Below you, swims fish so huge the shadow movement brings up fearful stories of your childhood of the great world spirits lurking deep below. Your great empire stretching to the ends of the earth with knowledge in mining, hunting, and sea travel at your back. Seeing the giant islands we now know as beautiful mountain ranges, wondering if they stretch below the wave tops forever. Wondering what is just through that narrow pass. Finding another lake and another, stretching deep into the western region we now call North America. Are you a giant to other men? Are you warring or traders? Do you have iron and bronze use before others; as such a technology that will be completely lost in the next 5,000 years to mankind. You have navigation skills and understanding of nature and the stars, able to travel great distances productively. Did you wonder if your legacy left carved into rocks a continent away from home would endure 20,000 years into the future?

CHRIS HEGG

Trade Routes

Following these lines of major petroglyph sites you soon see the trends and usefulness of the sites thousands of years ago. Now most are just random looking sites in the middle of dry desert valleys and passes. They still stand as usable today because there are still springs present, many lie within a mountain pass or valley entrance. The trending patterns of these large site locations follow the paths and interconnect where the gentlest and least distance paths go over land from one lake to the next. They existed so supplies and personnel can be moved the easiest. All trade paths funnel toward larger ports like Bishop and Coso Range, California. In these crossover regions existed large camps operated by the regional controller of the empire. Some regions were so large, covering hundreds of square miles, that there were many camps occupied shortly each year for gathering goods and full time occupation camps. This arrangement varied greatly and I find each new site yields a little more of the zones usage understanding. A camp's population had a variety of duties including moving cargo from one lake to another, boat repair, and operation. Trade supply storage and regional trade goods recovery and survival was another duty. Local goods included meat, hides, metals, minerals, wood, crops, sap, and a multitude of other items. Regional camps provided support to other regions in the form of supply sharing and additional military aid beyond defending their own zones. There is a problem with many of these camps however.

The concept you must consider while deciphering petroglyph map panels and trails is how the land WAS when the maps were made. There are three types of travel on the earth, land travel, water travel, and hybrid travel where both land and water travel are incorporated. Photo 208 is a visualization of the landmass black in contrast to the ancient lakes as blue with the white lines designating land travel paths. You must visualize the land masses 13,000 plus years ago to decide how the routes were established and linked to the petroglyphs.

ANCIENT UNIVERSAL LANGUAGE OF MAN

Photo 207 - Painting by Willow Phillips and Chris Hegg showing trading goods caravan leaving Lake Teals animal and goods transfer boats en route over Montgomery Pass to the Harbors at Bishop Ca. 16,000BP. An event played out all over the Great Basin during the time.

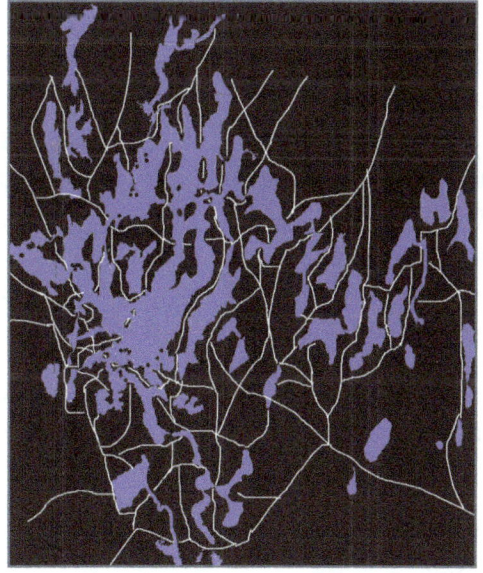

Photo 208 - Map drawn by author of general lake locations and trails around them.

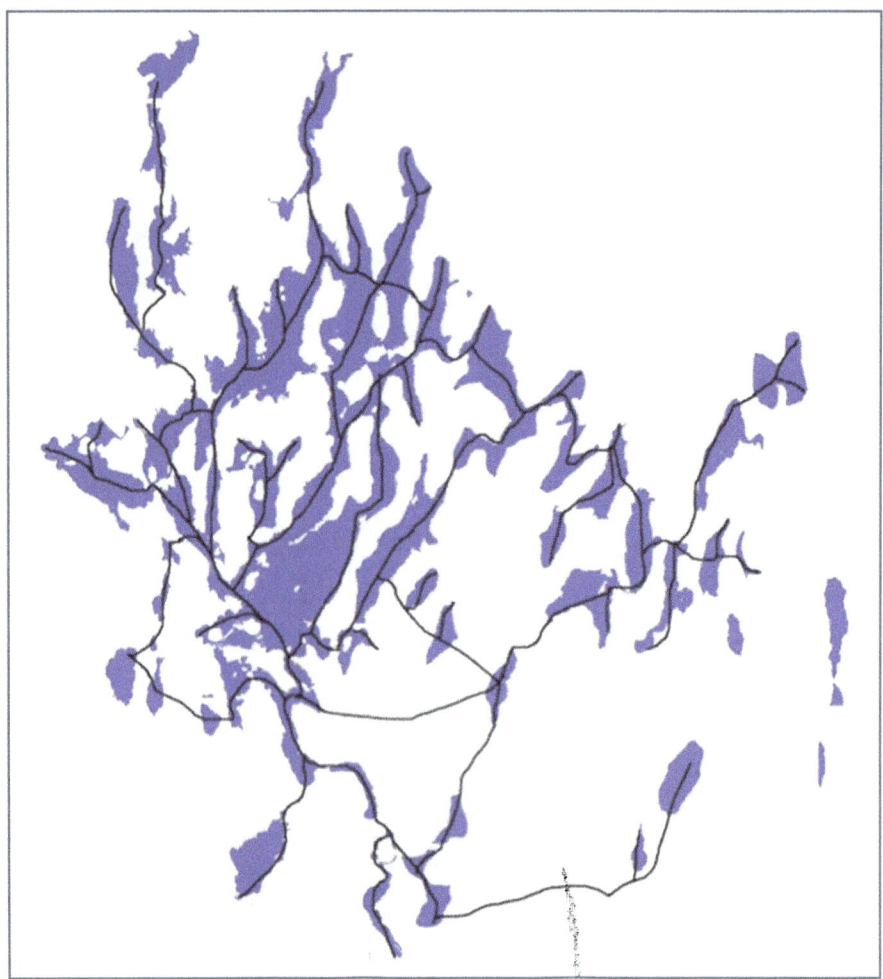

Photo 209 - Authors drawing of water paths on inland lakes in western U.S.A. territory today

    Photo 209 is Authors map reversal covering Nevada lakes (many more lakes spread into the interior of America) representing just some of the lakes and thus the water paths by boat primarily, with some land connections. Again note the routes they took, plus a hybrid routing over land, to complete certain journeys from one area to the next. Using the water paths as the main lanes of travel, only using land routes to move goods in the shortest of distances, was the way man has always incorporated trading the easiest and should be considered as the main way the ancients traveled whether it be war, trading, or exploration.

DEATH VALLEY GIANTS ACCOUNT

Another Indian account of this empire's arrival in Death Valley proper

This story from a Navaho Indian Oga-Make written in a spring 1948 issue of FATE Magazine.

... "Let us say that it is dusk in that strange place which you, the white-man, calls 'Death Valley.' I have passed tobacco...to the aged chief of the Paiutes who sits across a tiny fire from me and sprinkles corn meal upon the flames...

"The old chief looked like a wrinkled mummy as he sat there puffing upon his pipe. Yet his eyes were not those of the unseeing, but eyes which seemed to look back on long trails of time. His people had held the Inyo, Panamint and Death Valleys for untold centuries before the coming of the white-man. Now we sat in the valley which white-man named for Death, but which the Paiute calls Tomesha--The Flaming Land. Here before me as I faced eastward, the Funerals (mountains forming Death Valley's eastern wall) were wrapped in purple-blue blankets about their feet while their faces were painted in scarlet. Behind me, the Panamints rose like a mile-high wall, dark against the sinking sun.

"The old Paiute smoked my tobacco for a long time before he reverently blew the smoke to the four directions. Finally he spoke.

"'You ask me if we heard of the great silver airships in the days before white-man brought his wagon trains into the land?'

"'Yes grandfather, I come seeking knowledge.' (Among all tribes of my people, grandfather is the term of greatest respect which one man can pay to another.)

"'We, the Paiute Nation, have known of these ships for untold generations. We also believe that we know something of the people who fly them. They are called The Hav-musuvs.'

"'Who are the Hav-musuvs?'

"'They are a people of the Panamints, and they are as ancient as Tomesha itself.'

"He smiled a little at my confusion.

"'You do not understand? Of course not. You are not a Paiute. Then listen closely and I will lead you back along the trail of the dim past.

"'When the world was young, and this valley which is now dry, parched desert, was a lush, hidden harbor of a blue water- sea which *stretched from half way up those mountains to the Gulf of California, it is said that the Hav-musuvs came here in huge rowing-ships. They found great caverns in the Panamints, and in them they built one of their cities. At that time California was the island which the Indians of that state told the Spanish it was, and which they marked so on their maps.*

"'Living in their hidden city, the Hav-musuvs ruled the sea with their fast rowing-ships, trading with far-away peoples and bringing strange goods to the great quays said still to exist in the caverns.

"'Then as untold centuries rolled past, the climate began to change. The water in the lake went down until there was no longer a way to the sea. First the way was broken only by the southern mountains, over the tops of which goods could be carried. But as time went by, the water continued to shrink, until the day came when only a dry crust was all that remained of the great blue lake. Then the desert came, and the Fire-God began to walk across Tomesha, The Flaming-Land.

"'When the Hav-musuvs could no longer use their great rowing-ships, they began to think of other means to reach the world beyond. I suppose that is how it happened. We know that they began to use flying canoes. At first they were not large, these silvery ships with wings. They moved with a slight whirring sound, and a dipping movement, like an eagle.

"'The passing centuries brought other changes. Tribe after tribe swept across the land, fighting to possess it for awhile and passing like the storm of sand. In their mountain city still in the caverns, the Hav-musuvs dwelt in peace, far removed from the conflict. Sometimes they were seen in the distance, in their flying ships or riding on the snowy-white animals which took them from ledge to ledge up the cliffs. We have never seen these strange animals at any other place. To these people the passing centuries brought only larger and larger ships, moving always more silently.'

There is discussion of the sightings of UFOs prior to whites upon the continent yet the story again goes back to the ever present legends of great waterways across the western U.S. valleys that dried up and of settlers from distant lands. Specifically thru DEATH VALLEY and beyond. The only obstacle between the waters is the mountain range.

[Source: http://www.archaeology.org/issues/145-1409/features/2367-peopling-the-americas-paradigms writes about man in America 13,000 years ago and states; *"Clovis is still important,"... "but we have to realize that there were people here before. Now we have to determine how long before Clovis people were here, who they were, what kind of technology they carried, and how they migrated through the continent and settled the empty landscapes."* says Mike Waters, director of the Center for the Study of the First Americans at Texas A&M University.]

LAKES OF ANCIENT TIMES

Scientific disciplines often stand in conflict with one another on multiple topics. Even within their own disciplines separate theories conflict with each other. The time of the petroglyph first use around the inland lakes, possibly 20,000 years ago, was before the age of surviving historical records. The ancient lake system in the United States west allowed for free movement of trading goods over them to the oceans and beyond via interconnected channels from one lake to the next. We will take a look at the elevations and lake shapes now.

> Columbus.Edu website states *"During the last glacial period, the U.S. Great Basin experienced much greater effective precipitation, allowing lakes to fill most of its subbasins (lower figure). The largest of these lakes was Lake Bonneville..... second largest being Lake Lahontan...., a lake at the northeastern edge of the Great Basin that was approximately the size of modern Lake Michigan. Though Lake Bonneville's history has been studied for over a century, substantial uncertainties remain about the precise timing and rate of the lake's rise and fall and the lake's response to the abrupt climate changes of the last glacial period."*

Excerpt from a great detailed report of the full extent of the lake system throughout ancient Nevada located at http://water.nv.gov/mapping/chronologies/walker/part2.cfm

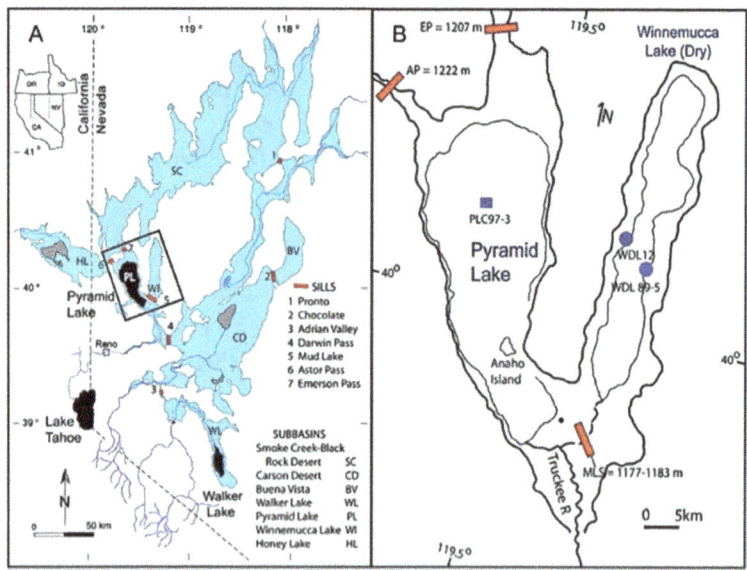

Photo 211 - Maps by Benson L., Hattori E., Southon J., Aleck B Map from 2013: *Dating North America's oldest petroglyphs, Winnemucca Lake subbasin, Nevada, Journal of Archaeological Science*, vol. 40, no. 12, pp. 4466–4476; doi: 10.1016/j.jas.2013.06.022 showing the oldest proven dated petroglyph locations (area now closed indefinitely due to media attention of findings drawing many rock thieves to the sites caught with chisels and power rock saw equipment trying to chop the symbols off the rocks recently.)

75,000-10,000 Years Ago

"... as recently as 12,500 years ago, that much of the area now contained within the upper Carson River Basin was covered in snowpack and glaciers.... Lake Lahontan, along with Lake Bonneville, which covered northwestern Utah and parts of eastern Nevada, represented the Great Basin's major Ice Age lakes which inundated vast portions of Nevada and Utah. .... only the Great Salt Lake remains as a reminder of the prehistoric presence of Lake Bonneville, and only Pyramid Lake and Walker Lake remain as major lake remnants of Lake Lahontan.

Lake Lahontan experienced several peaking enlargements ... as recently as 12,500 years ago, ... attained a maximum surface elevation of approximately 4,380 feet above mean sea level (MSL), and reached a maximum depth of at least 886 feet.... the north-south extent of Lake Lahontan stretched from just below the Nevada-Oregon border in the *north to just south of Walker Lake to present-day Hawthorne, Nevada.... Lake Lahontan also extended well up the lower Truckee River canyon towards... the present-day City of Reno (near the Court of Antiquity site) near Lagomarsino Canyon (a site of another petroglyph group*

14,000-12,500 Years Ago

Lake Lahontan and Walker Lake underwent their last highstands or peaking enlargements. Throughout the Great Basin, Lake Lahontan rose to an elevation of approximately 4,370 feet MSL ... all seven major sub-basins.... of Lake Lahontan—(1) Smoke Creek/Black Rock Desert; (2) Carson Desert; (3) Buena Vista; (4) Walker Lake; (5) Pyramid Lake; (6) Winnemucca Dry Lake; and (7) Honey Lake--were connected.(10)

Excerpt from State of Nevada Division of Water Resources webpage. (Proven evidence of Nevada lacustrine basin petroglyphs being aged at as far back as possibly 14,800 years ago now exists by the Desert Research Institute on a study of a Pyramid Lake panel).

Much data can be found on websites like the Desert Research Institue (www.DRI.Edu) for water level research, the following is an abstract from the website list of research papers.

U.S. Geological Survey Water Resources Investigations Report 85-4262, 14 p. *"The last high lake level (highstand) of Pleistocene Lake Lahontan occurred 14,000 to 12,500 years before present.....Only when lake level exceeds 1,308 meters, does Lake Lahontan become a single body of water, that acts in a unified manner to changes in the regional hydrologic balance...."* Benson, L. V., and Mifflin, M. D., 1986, Reconnaissance bathymetry of basins occupied by Pleistocene Lake Lahontan, Nevada and California

Geological Society of America Abstracts with Programs, v. 22, no. 7, p. 253. states *"Surface areas of lakes in the Lahontan and Bonneville basins increased by a factor of ~9 to 10 between 30,000 and 14,000 yr B.P ... In southern Nevada, the last interval of significant ground-water recharge occurred between 18,000 and 9,000 yr B.P. These changes in the ..Great Basin appear related to the changing size of the continental ice sheet and to the return .... to a glacial mode -10,500 yr B.P. (Younger Dryas climatic event)..."*

Benson, L. V., Hostetler, S. W., and Giorgi, F., 1990, Climate induced variation in the hydrologic balances of Lake Lahontan and Lake Bonneville during the past 25,000 years.

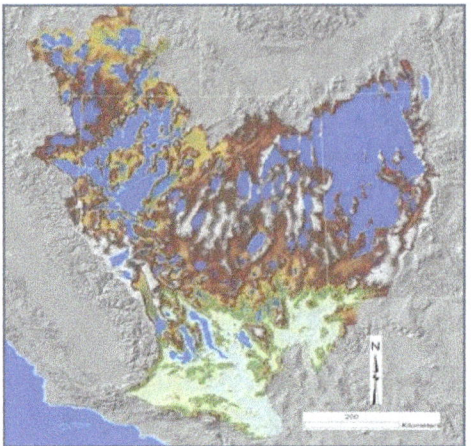

Photo 212 - Map showing high water region with permission by Ken Adams, Desert Research Institute, http://www.DRI.edu/ken-adams

Photo 213 - Author's Photo of a sign at Red Rock Pass, the location of a giant natural dam that breached letting waters flood into the Nevada/Utah areas within weeks. Geologic site evidence of how the lake levels could attain such heights 13,000-20,000 years ago or at anytime without precipitation changes.

Site Location

Author's map in electronic Photo 214 of possible target location drawing to assist in finding petroglyph sites within a region. Focusing on locations of mountain ridges coming closest to the ancient lake level is the prime spots where petroglyph sites are located for the lake trade routes. Factors must be included to deduce other variables that are important in a site location, mainly fresh water. Any springs, rivers, deltas and canyons accessible to the lake adds to better target solutions. The best sites for lake panels will be geographical ends of the lake, where lower elevation passes to the next valley

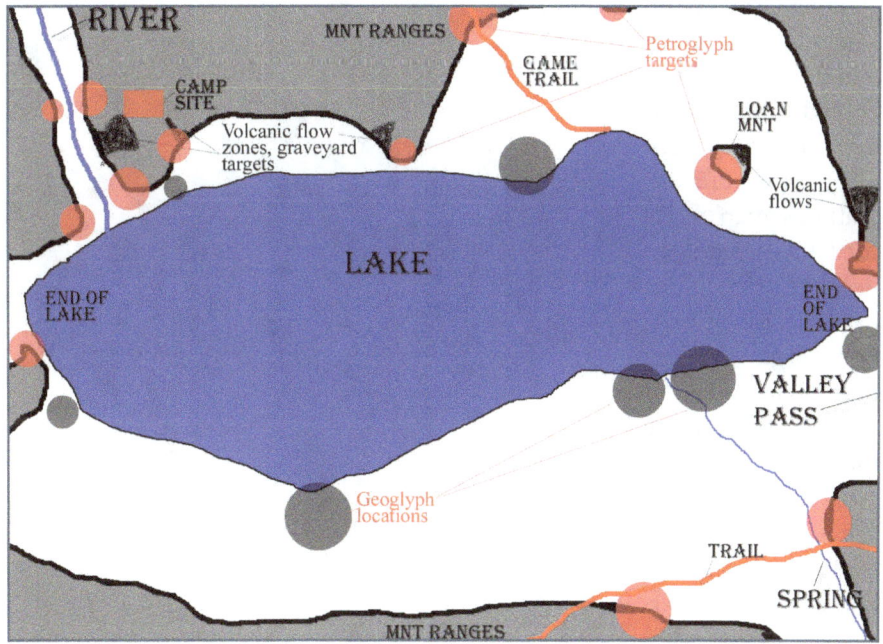

Photo 214 - Map drawn by Author.

or lake exists. From that point search springs and other freshwater sources, caves, flat areas that could have camps. Those closest to the lake ends will have petroglyph sites.

Other hunting specific sites will be along animal trail tight areas, near springs or river edges where rock comes closest to the water edge or crosses it. Above these areas are best found campsites, where trails will lead down to the water and hunt sites. Along these trails look for graveyard petroglyph sites and sometimes usage petroglyph sites for growing crops, hunting and other resource panels explaining information such as seasonal fish spawning, migrations, sap gathering, trade goods movements and ship repair and harbor sites. The more multiples in one spot in the valley the higher the target probability will exist. Note volcanic detritus piles along hill edges where graveyards exist. War sites could include a graveyard that would not otherwise be where it should due to the nature of war happening where it happens. Usually graveyards mean camps and trade route locations. Geoglyphs will be along the edges of the ancient lake level. Loan hills and mountains close to or that were islands in the ancient lakes are high target zones for obvious reasons. They usually make coves and safe harbors and provide higher visible elevations to build and keep protective forces and light fires for night navigation and emergency response. Many floating cities and outposts are anchored near such islands and close hills.

Photo 215 is Author's map modified to include red dots as target locations for possible large trading petroglyph sites at various lake shore locations thru west Nevada. Note; there are intentional deceptions in actual correlations to existing sites, presented

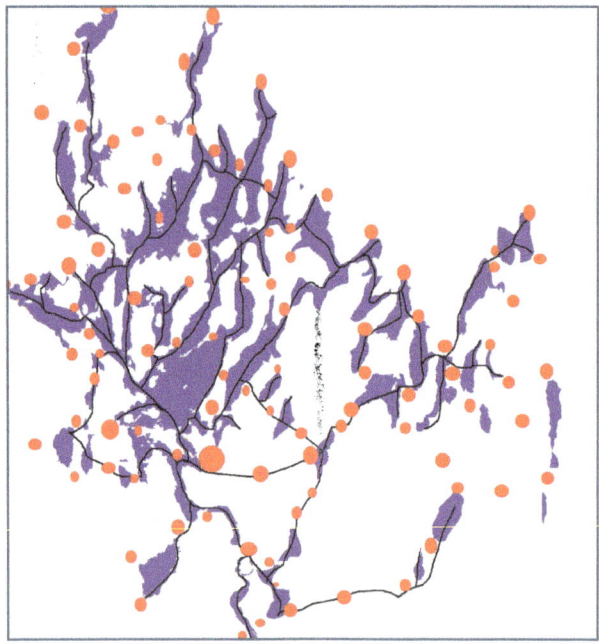

Photo 215 - Map of petroglyph site distribution in relation to trade good movement paths both on the lake and overland. Referenced sites and site sizes are not based off of actual sites! [Source: Author]

to display the way to target locating these petroglyph sites by you, using ancient lake level maps generated by you and others.

Known petroglyph sites throughout the central Western Nevada region comprising of over 25 large petroglyph sites within 100 miles of each other are located in the elevation 3994-4350 level. Other zones have site ranges that vary no more than 100 ft as well. All above the high water marks of 20-12 ka times. Note some lakes come so close in many regions that it is obvious trading goods transfer locations or ancient modified paths with possible ditches dug so interconnections could exist for the ease of transporting goods and pulling boats across from lake to lake. Just like today man was smart and used pack animals including elephants (see elephant chapter) to carry goods across land. Pack paths and other types of paths, like defense paths for wartime efforts, exist at sites.

Today, there are numerous large geoglyph rock alignment symbols located for miles around these ancient shorelines. Some designs appear to be visible from height only, and have data characteristics indicative to possible ancient hang gliding practice of flight. How is it that large Universal Language petroglyph sites are present in every ancient lakeside shore location across the western states of the U.S. and not below the ancient lake levels if they are not of the era of the ancient lakes? Five sites point to coincidence, but every large site throughout the states located precisely at the lake shores certainly proves this point more than the no evidence approach of modern archaeological science saying the sites are mostly "hunting magic sites" of recent design! At least geology and simplistic usability ideas can be attached to my theory. Attaching an extremely laborious activity, practiced everywhere with inconceivable symmetry and harmony of symbology, across a swath of regions influenced by drugs as a taught and obeyed scientific notion simply makes me laugh...out...loud. John C. Fremont quoted in his reports to congress in 1846 during his encounter with the Walker Lake Paiutes for the first time that they were beat back to barbarians. Running around barely clothed eating live lizards off rocks. They had stacked Bighorn Sheep skulls in piles facing the mountain range as some type of religious effort, maybe for hunting. Does it seem to you like this effort coincides with hungrily hiking to useless areas away from game (say near a dried up ancient lake shores) and spending great effort carefully carving intricate designs, in similarity with other global symbology, just so some magic event will happen where food will fall in your lap? A better use of energy is obviously spent eating live lizards off rocks.

CHRIS HEGG

Lake Petroglyphs

Let us shed for a moment the blanket of academic denial of smart men living more than 300 years ago and open our collective minds to the possibility that humans could actually wipe their own behinds successfully before Universities existed. This story begins at the great inland lakes we have discussed. These major petroglyph sites were needed for navigation through the empire of the Ancients. At certain locations existed larger boat docks with images of viking style sailing ships with sails and oars and long boats in

Photo 216 - Petroglyph site, Bishop, California [Source: Author]

smaller lake locations. Pillars and fire pits lit the way for navigating treturous waters in all kinds of bad weather. Some sites included cargo manifests and sometimes probably reviled at new goods never before seen and were written for historical significance. The new invent of Super Maze as the future crop to end starvation might have been one commodity reviled. Major cargo losses, war raiding, and unknown loss mysteries are also written as witness and information in later disputes for tracking such trading cycles.

The Author's photo of petroglyph site in Photo 216, Bishop, California, showing the cargo manifests of many ships lost (upside down ships images) in storms due to this rock structure that stuck out of the water near a major port in those days. Lake travel is notorious for large waves in bad weather, emergency landing locations must have been well known and maps of the lakes showing details like this rock structure were probably shared among captains by the regional leaders order. A large naval battle was had here between a raiding nation and is also documented on this outcrop.

The Author's photo of Viking long boat (Photo 217) at the protected harbor with a maze symbol designating the cargo. Standing at the height of the harbor cove exists this style ship with oars, dragon brow, and sails (or a large load of cargo outlined in squares to show lot amounts). The cargo of maze and beans seen in plant form to the right. The top cover over the sails is the night sky and the many X symbols of the stars. Probably the first seeds on the continent.

Photo 217 - Viking long boat at the protected harbor

Photo 218 - Author's photos of the harbor face showing the rows of ship masts crammed into the cove.

Photo 219 - Rendition by Willow Phillips and Chris Hegg of the Bishop Harbor 16,000 years ago with ancient ships at anchor trading supplies.

Photo 220 - Author's photo of the Biship Harbor now, in the middle of a dry landscape hundreds of miles from the sea.

Photo 221 shows a modern chub fishing boat in decay in just tens of years behind Walker Lake, Nevada, at the historic fish company dock location built of rock walls. Given 500 more years, much less 15,000 years, there will be nothing left of this debris. The reason for this, like in history, natural building supplies are used, decaying in short time naturally. Even metals will decay in that period. The technology in this boat's design for wood is impressive, yet will vanish not long in the future. Note the distance of this dock to the existing level of the lake today in just modern times.

Photo 221 - Decaying boat [Source: Author]

Modern Thoughts

Conventional thinking says nobody existed in America prior to Clovis People and any ancient could not even build a good boat to take advantage of lakes or oceans and thus remained in a stooped over position wielding a wooden club walking everywhere on the planet. Even though cultures everywhere sailed to unimaginable regions on the globe and built pyramids of rock aligned to the invisible North Pole. What is agreed upon is that Columbus sailed to North America in HOPES there was something there—Vikings coming before him—by boat as well. The realization that 50 million tons of mined copper vanished from the Great Lakes before the white man is even more compelling. The realization that great expanses of time masks human visitations is easier for me to believe than otherwise desolate petroglyph sites being accidentally dispersed around ancient lake shores hundreds of square miles long with matching elevations.

Pointer

Another symbol panel that appears so insignificant like in Photo 222, yet was vital to finding a hidden cave at a location today called Grimes Point near Fallon, Nevada (a petroglyph park worth visiting). There are a vast amount of petroglyph areas located around the mountain range and many caves, but to date, only Hidden Cave was hidden and contained vast amounts of Indian artifacts. Many vanished after the cave was discovered by a group of kids playing rock fights and felt the cool air between two rocks. The cave was so hidden that reoccupation groups needed to find it again and again and so used an indicator. But to have such a treasure as a hidden cave is vital for your survival and control of an area, allowing you a location to hide, store goods, and weapons and must not fall into the wrong hands when you are not present! So how do you accomplish this, showing a marker to find it yet hide it from your enemies? You conceal the marker in plain view, that's how. You do this by placing the marker on it's own, away from the main panels of interest, so anyone not exactly knowing your total Universal Language language will never find it or pass right by it as human nature focuses on the big bold and beautiful panels elsewhere.

Photo 223 is the "look here" symbol used in sign and another example of the circle. A rough white drawing of the pointing index finger and open gap between the outstretched thumb (right hand) is directed toward the cave opening as you would use your hand in sign language to tell the viewer to look in the direction your hands finger and thumb point toward in Photo 223. At the top of the finger it ends with the tip as an open circle with the opening

Photo 222 - Petroglyph photo unaltered [Source: Author]

Photo 223A - Symbol highlighted for clarity

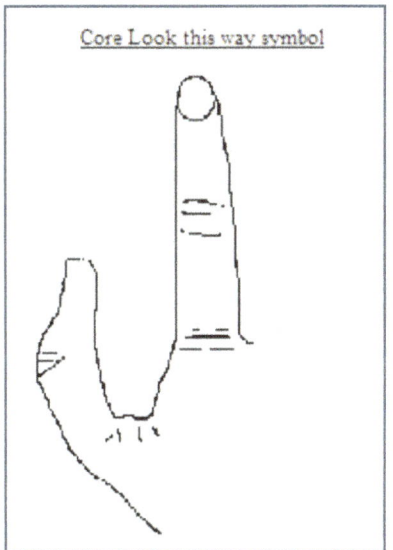

Photo 223B - Symbol drawn in sign language hand position for clarity

toward the cave entrance. If you look at the original Photo 224, you can see a natural ridge of the rock where this circle exists and a small notch taken out of it dead center. If you bend down and look up the finger you will notice there are two notches removed in the rock, one at the top of the rocks edge where more symbol work was done to designate using rock incorporation that the cave is "up on the cliff." The notches can be lined up like gun sights

Photo 224 - Target relation to cave entrance with line drawn through gun sights of symbol on panel as human-modified rock incorporation [Source: Author]

and you are looking directly at the cave entrance, now completely visible with a generator shed sitting at it's left and a dirt pile from the cave entrance being dug out and inside excavated. Photo 224 is the greatest example of how important the smallest symbol is and indicates true rock incorporation. They centered the image on the rock and the finger extends upward (as the cave is upward). The top edge of the rock is worked to show that high up is what they are talking about (distance to the cave is over 600 ft). They used the natural ridges and chipped in precise notches to allow lineup to find the cave with the assistance of someone on the cliff they can direct to the entrance. The fact that they drew the hand in elaborate 2D styling shows time was taken to make this a perfect glyph hidden in plain sight. No other glyph is nearby and this is centered in the valley ringed with glyphs.

As seen in Photo 225, here is a look inside a portion of the Hidden Cave excavated when I revisited in 2013. When I was a child visiting in the 80s only half way down was dug and they ran out of visible evidence and claimed the occupation was only up to 1500 years ago. Then they realized the flowing of flood dirt into the cave was not uniform and kind of rounded as it filled and that the edges, though thinner, represented larger layering in the center so they dug deeper past a dead zone, and guess what? They are now going further and further back in time, past 12,000 years. A trip to the Carson City Museum will give you examples of many of the items found here including intricate nets.

Photo 225 - Inside Hidden Cave, Fallon, Nv. Grimes Point State Archeological Park. Much can be seen now that scholars dug deeper and realized much older occupation existed.

Through petroglyph decipherment in this valley I have determined there are two more smaller hidden caves! I used an expensive treasure hunting magnetic gauss detector that can pickup cavities in the earth, up to several hundred feet on the tops of the cliffs, toward the south of Hidden Cave and discovered two: one a cavity and the other a tunnel leading through my scan field at a depth of 15-30 ft. The larger cavity is approx 25 ft round in the scan field and keeps going.

Photo 226 is Author's scan image, The cave cavity seen outlined in a white line, blue being the most northern toward the cliff and should be the entrance. I was 35 feet back from the cliff face and no exposure of a cave exists due to detritus along the cliff face.

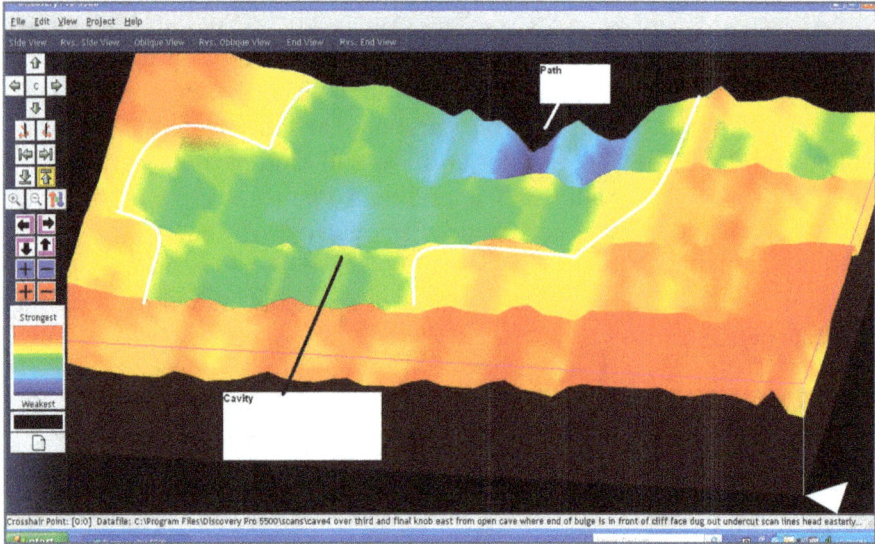

Photo 226 - RF trough showing a cavity that may be showing possible second hidden cave location underground at Hidden Cave [Source: Author using a Deep Scan Discovery treasure detector]

In Photo 227 you can clearly see the blue depression indicated going right through the middle of my scan field. The wave patterns along the path are from my pace on the mountain as the detector detects the short delays and walking motions and 4 paths were done. The W shape of the blue designates the highest rise, though it could be ever so slight, in the center of the cavity. In this case, it is somewhat narrow, but has pockets to each side and so the real cavity probably undulates wildly on the floor going from wide enough to enter to very thin. Wave action at this height of the ancient lake bore the caves by undermining the volcanic contact and later man probably widened the caves by removing what they could in cobble and sands. More work with BLM to attempt discovery still follows, but I hope to prove the caves do exist and were used by ancient man.

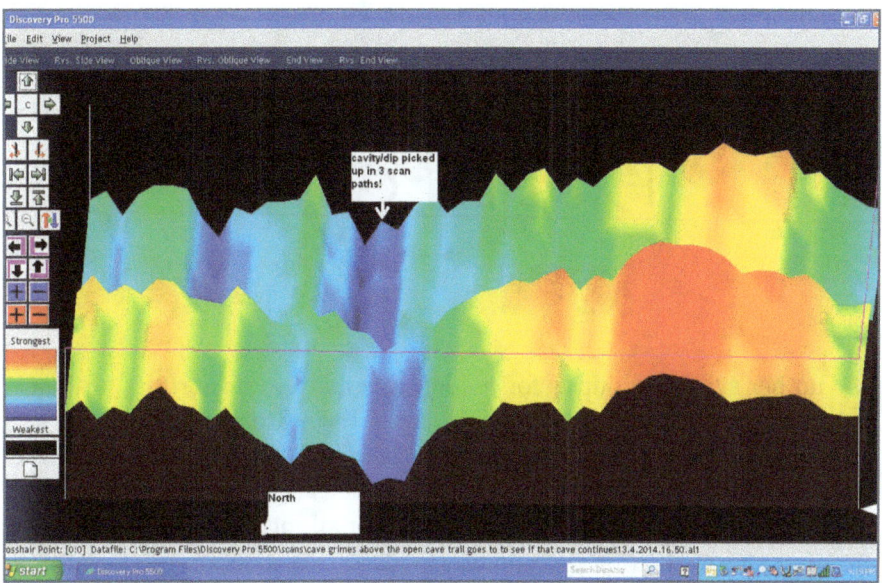

Photo 227 - Thinner entrance detected more down range for a possible third hidden cave [Source: Author]

Hidden Caves

Another symbol group is for hidden caves, a resource crutial to the existence of the empire in foreign lands trying to keep control of vast networks of lake accessible resources others would surely attempt to sneak in and steal. Normal caves are different as they are large, visible, and compromisable. Hidden includes another concept all together to relate the cave meaning and sometimes incorporates normal cave symbology around it as clues. As seen with micro-decipherment, hidden caves are the most important well guarded secret of the ancients. These sites allowed greater usefulness of the regional resources because the retreat could be hidden, keep supplies stored longer, and afford protection of the people. Most large petroglyph sites are located within a zone of hidden caves for this reason. I must exclude the understanding of all concepts of the following symbol groups for obvious reasons to avoid these resources from being found. Without thorough knowledge of how the ancients keyed the panel information, simply knowing the symbol meaning will be of no use actually finding the caves without the other decipherment. Since modern archeology again and again has already disproved petroglyphs as a language in the thousands of man hour papers, books, and lectures, there really would be no harm; but I will exclude them anyways. Archeologists can not provide locations to these vast sites, yet the petroglyph Universal Language can.

Lizards

The Universal Language is based heavily off of nature and about one third is represented in idiograph format (symbols representing concepts) as described earlier. We see this in the human movements, environment mimicking like the fall of rain drops and in animal use. So it is no surprise that there are many animal symbols in Universal Language and the meanings relate to the animals familiar ACTIONS that it performs in certain situations that other animals/mammals do not; to reference the human actions of the panel story. Thinking from your own knowledge we know that herds of quadrupeds migrate and move together, so it is used to represent motion. We know that if a bird is approached it... flies. So it is used to depict flight and flight in the presence of danger. And if you spook a lizard where does it go? Under rocks and tight areas! Thus the lizard symbol is used for hidden caves.

As seen in Photos 228-233, a small representation of the many hidden cave lizard symbols to numerous to show just within the Nevada desert alone. It is interesting to note that when you hunt for petroglyph sites you will usually

Photo 228 - 233 - Compiled photos by Author showing distributed lizard symbols denoting the many hidden caves that exist throughout the world.

always find real lizards on the panels and not so much away from panel areas. Coincidence or keepers of the sites?

Author's Photo 234 of a great example of the symbol used in a close proximity format (looking more like a mouse) near Hidden Cave in Grimes Point Park near Fallon, Nevada, with Hidden Cave gate and generator house at the cave entrance in the background. There are two other smaller hidden caves located here still undiscovered that I show the magnetic gauss scanning of in this book.

Photo 234 - Modified symbol to hidden cave
[Source: Author]

Photo 235 - A second panel denoting hidden caves. [Source: Author]

Photo 236 - Author's photo of a hidden cave complex having 7 caves.

Photo 237 - Author's photo inside one hidden cave opened up.

THEMES

I end here showing some sagas our ancestors encountered. As my purpose of this book was to focus on the teaching of the Universal Language symbols, the key to deciphering the sites out there, I refrained from digging into the depths of the stories told. I believe your research will best be fulfilled in the Universal Language by knowing these details of decipherment where you are able to read your own interpretations and not having them done where confusions or nuances are lost due to me telling the stories. I plan on future books expanding on advanced petroglyph understanding and telling some stories of mankind's past. As so many more symbols and groups are on the drawing board for decipherment there is much to learn and write about; but I have covered many of the most important symbols used throughout the world.

In closing I would like to expand on a few fascinating stories told from the people who labored so meticulously to create the sites so those stories may be kept forever, hoping they would be unlocked in some distant future. Nothing grabs our collective imaginations more than events that happened to man in the past. Those trying and brutal days long past, wrought with dangers from every direction. In the hopes of getting just a tiny glimpse into a time where almost nothing is known like traveling back in a time machine. These stories are just the start of a vast connected network of history written on the very stones we live on, in every Continent! My hope is that you take this knowledge and venture out to find your own stories of the past.

Snake and Tarantula Harvesting and War

Some of the greatest adventures of man happened long before mankind's current documented achievements. In the days of ancients there existed some very harrowing jobs people today would consider insane. One being the rattlesnake migration harvesting event. Every year the Spring migrations of rattlesnakes in Mineral County existed clear up until modern times. My late Grandfather first came to Hawthorne, Nevada, around 1952 and as they were coming around the lake in Spring a rattlesnake migration was happening and hundreds were crossing the highway and his station wagon got a flat. He took it into the local gas station and the owner ran his hand inside the tire to find the object and his hand got punctured by rattlesnake fangs broke off into the tire. His hand swelled and a hospital visit was required.

Decades prior, a team was attempting to dig a stagecoach stop water well in this very canyon, but every time they exploded dynamite to sink the shaft rattlesnakes inundated the crew and made them run for their lives. The well was finished by hand due to the problem. Prior to this 16,000 years, I can imagine the first humans to witness this natural movement of snakes was a group probably camping near these giant rocks due to the spring being nearby and somewhere in early sunset the massive bodies of thousands of rattlesnakes were heard scurrying out of their hibernation caves located here and

Photo 238 - Ancient war rock [Source: Author]

moving into the sleeping camp. Whereby I am sure all of the group ended up on top of the rocks to wait out the night in terror of being bitten! Since then it appears the site was popular to them.

    Author's Photo 238 is designated by me as the "War Rock" as evidence by the path of war above the top of the rock panel, depicting a force of another group coming from the ridges down into the canyon, a superior force against this smaller group of Si-Te-Ca warrior giants (shown below) in the canyon. But the superior group was defeated by the smaller group and thus boasted about heavily. The group surviving the attack would only write of defeat of a superior number and the story was grand enough to be displayed in this massive marker panel that again resembles a massive snake head, probably the local groups mascot due to the rattlesnake harvesting during migration here yearly. Notice again the long path line disconnected from the downward facing arrow points to clearly designate this path. Seen below the path of war is the lower "teeth" which are the smaller human force who "defends" against this attack. The human form is molded into a defense symbol where the body is an arrowhead pointing down and bracketed on both top and bottom with a horizontal path lines, the arms to show "bar or block" the war path from above and thus showing defiance against its point by removing the sharper portion of the tip toward the bottom and attaching "surprised" legs pointing straight out. The symbol combination of defenders then keeps the human form in a shape similar to warriors with raised spears while incorporating all the added information of what they were doing. Lined up correctly using rock incorporation as this rock shape has a curved outward arch at the top the war path is drawn upon. The curvature continues down to where the small defending party is, but added together right makes a fantastic artistic resemblance of a snake head, which is the main site use beyond tarantula harvesting. Even the moon lit heads of the army shown below the moon is made into a snake form, probably more to depict what they thought of them doing this sneak action than anything else.

    Along the same lines as the last story, this very same place has another secret—hard learned I assure you! It is the secret that once again this entire region is one of the largest migration paths for tarantulas in autumn. The migrations were so huge in my little town of Luning north of here you could not walk down the road sometimes and driving was like riding on a black sea of fur. Once again I am positive another group, assured of no rattlesnake migrations within the start of Autumn had a peaceful camp of solitude and rest until somewhere in the night a solid mass of strange scraping tips and scurries awoke them to find the area consumed with moving spiders. Spiders so large they doubled the size of today's tasty treat eaten as a delicatessen around the world in many countries...the tarantulas! Once again the night screams of everyone scrambling for the safety of the tops of the rocks as shelter echoed in the canyon as torches were lit and defendable areas were made to protect them through the night. The migrations would again be a yearly mainstay of diet and trading harvesting of now two precious commodities.

The ancient's Chief died here during this raid and a panel (Photo 3) is dedicated to him. Photo 238 shows that nothing much matches my general rock layout. There is weather at the bottom, war data in the center and the "eye" of the artistic snake is the full moon. Under the eye exists the "line of men's heads" who attacked them, shown marching and viewed from the moonlight.

Photo 239 - Snake harvest panel on reverse side of war rock. [Source: Author]

At the reverse side of the war rock (Photo 239) exists the season symbol with the rattlesnake scales background. To the side exists several of the harvesting operations to herd the snakes, seen from the top.

Photo 240 is Author's photo of more activity of the processing of snakes including stretching and drying.

Authors Photo 241 of the skinners or tanners pulling skin from the insides. The group of 4 shown hard at work on the worktop segmenting certain parts and piling in baskets in a type of assembly line. Remember this era of rattlesnakes were no small critters! Being far in excess of 6 foot each of these harvests provided massive amounts of tradable goods.

Photo 240 - Snake processing panel including drying skins [Source: Author]

Photo 241 - Workers processing snakes on the rock [Source: Author]

Earthquake Camp

Author's Photo 242 of a site located between the inland great lake complex of western Nevada and the Montgomery pass beside the White Mountains where supplies had to be transported by land over the pass down to the large volcanic coves, used as trading docks, at Bishop, California. The stopover site here had water in the form of a large year round spring and shelter consisting of a large overhanging volcanic tuft shelf in a wash. The area is near what is now called the Mina Deflection. A group of three faults that transfer thrust energy from the Owens Valley, Long Valley faults to the Walker Lane fault area in the vicinity of Hawthorne, Nevada. Many earthquakes have happened here and this was no exception in historic times. So violent the thrusts a friend and I experienced a quake when I was 18 while walking out of the hills after breaking down. We walked all day and finally at 9:00 pm we could see the lights of Mina so we took a break. While we were sitting on the graded bank on the side of the dirt road, an earthquake thrust threw us on our backs. But before we hit our backs, an opposite thrust happened and flung us forward almost hitting our faces. But again, while we were in forward flight, almost ready to touch knees to dirt, the ground flung back and sat us directly upright like nothing happened. This all happened before we could even respond with our arms to block the impacts! We figured after that we actually remained in place and the ground is what moved? We both looked at each other in

Photo 242 - Zoomed area of main panel depicting earthquake intensity [Source: Author]

surprise and quickly jumped up and never sat down until we made it to Mina some 6 miles ahead, feeling and hearing tremors the entire way! It was a 7.4 epicenter right where we were. Here is my telling of the story written on the petroglyph panels with the facts I deciphered from the panels and from what I know about the area, earthquakes, their culture, and the panel details.

[At dawn, after our first nights stay here, we awoke to a deafening noise! As we travelled south toward the shores of the great long lake, our great mother earth had unleashed her mighty power on us! During the journey to and from the lakes carrying supplies we stopped here to rest and water, and sing goodbyes when the fading warmth of the autumn comes and we leave for the winter; in celebration to our most sacred of grounds we call the highlands. From the south we traveled in great caravans, ever increasing, to this land as our daring forefathers have for centuries. We left our villages across the seas to come to the new land, for here lies the wealth of our empire, our stronghold from intruders, and our new home. We have met several cultures in these lands to the rising sun. They were apart (independent groups) and without (a language and trading value) until we taught them. We are the teachers of the language that covers the world. Now we have many friends who travel great distances by boat to visit and learn more of the world's way. Here is one of our meeting places, used sometimes as great beginnings to other tribes they bring. It is sometimes here we teach those who come. We teach our language, the universal language that makes all trading and brotherhood possible. We teach our math and our navigation so they can also learn to cross the mother world to distant lands like ours.

But this morning a tragic day was to be born of blood and death, there would be prayer and sorrow and the skies would be filled with the smoke of our brothers as their spirits were carried away in the winds. This spot is sacred, as the great mother has unleashed furies before on our people since the beginning, but none like this.

The mother rolled and buckled. Huge waves of land came from the North and caught us lumbering in the shadows of the cliffs. No man or animal stood with the waves. Loud snaps came as the cliff rocks broke loose and fell on man and animal alike. Great rolls toward the south fled away underground like the underworld rose to eat us. The animals fled, and fell into cracks like open mouths from below, blowing large plumes of dust as they breathed out and closed their lips. Five times the ground lifted us up as it rolled south, twisting backward like an ocean wave until we fell again and again. The sun was blocked out by dust everywhere and the noise of the fishers screaming and the mountains groaning made us cower in fear. When the dust settled and all stood still the ground was cracked everywhere. Our cliff's ledge was broken and lying on our sons and our wives and animals were missing everywhere.

Screams filled the valley as the swampy marsh and grasses were scoured by survivors looking for loved ones. Many were safe, but some were never found, feared swallowed up by the mother herself.

There were some half eaten, animals with parts sticking up from the ground, bloody and still. More waves came as the day went on, others running back who were on the search for animals (who had ran off) came back saying they could see the ground waves coming toward us far off in the distance before we ever heard it or felt it. The smaller worlds below visited and could be felt riding by toward the south, pushing ground due north under our feet in harsh shoves. We moved to the top of the ridges on the flat areas to avoid the swallowing of the ground and the marsh waters flowing to our camp below. We performed the ceremonies needed to send our loved ones to the winds and awaited the next day, before traveling back the way we came to the satellite graveyard, where our other loved ones were buried in the sacred rock. We performed the cremation there, where trees were plentiful, before returning to this spot to gather our goods and finish our journey south. We would return to them next season to gather their spirits and move them to the sacred resting place on the great island (central mountains).

Our elephants were intact, losing none, as they were well outside the falling rock area and headed to high ground far before the shaking started. We believe they know when the mother will shake. They helped us several times through the day. Our trade supplies survived, though we did not care at the time. In sorrow we write this story for others who follow, beware the mother's fury here!]

Photo 243 - Author's photo of more data along the wall designating unusual symbols meant for another book. Known as "Shields" due to resemblance in many references I can assure you they are not!

Rose Bush Site

Photo 244 shows a keystone that was a confusing petroglyph site when I was a boy, but I spent many a spring, summer, and fall here camping and fishing I was finally able to realize I witnessed firsthand the confirmation I needed to begin my decipherment of these petroglyphs.

Photo 244 - Photo of Author and season symbol.

The site has the largest Season symbol group I've seen, mostly made from the natural rock incorporation in a spectacular display. The images were so large I could not find the theme symbol while present at the site, only after I got home and opened up the images I took did I recognize it. You will see it to the right of the season and in the top image of this story. The theme is always an artistic representation of the object discussed on the panels.

Authors Photo 245, over zoomed to match but probably the best way to show it as comparison. It is a rather large representation of the head and wings of the Monarch Butterfly. This site confused me until I remembered every year I would see the coming and going of migrations of these butterflies by the hundreds of thousands. One morning I woke up and went out fishing from the camp trailer early and there were so many on the wild rose bushes you could not see the bush under it. They stretched for miles upstream clear to

Photo 245 - Author's photo of front facing keystone panel.

this point. By the time the sun rose, I was not 100 yards from this glyph and they all took off flying away. Within minutes I was scrambling for my life as the air was filled with so many I could not see and soon was inhaling them. I had to hide my face in my shirt for over a half hour as they gained elevation and finally cleared the bushes enough for me to stand up and uncover. I did not know they migrated or transformed there until many decades later, I just thought they roamed around and rose bushes were an obvious butterfly attraction. Now I know this is one of the crucial migration stopovers along their journeys North and South. Little destinations are known along the various Migrations paths and ongoing research is filling most of those gaps.

Photo 246 - Monarch head and front of wings to show similarity to "theme image" on Photo 245 [Source: Author]

Photo 247 - Authors modified photo to show natural (white by human hands, black is natural and natural modified by humans)

Photo 247 shows the lines drawn in on authors photo, showing both natural and human made, depicting migration patterns. One of the best representations of rock incorporation, and more importantly, just how much nature seems to provide a story rock already representing the story. The combination of nature to the Universal Language must have relayed a great sense of harmony and symbiosis to the writer to be part of. Tattooing use in this instance could also be said. This symbol of autumn could include summer. The outlined human shadow lines radiating would determine exactly what dates and combinations exist but such research has not been completely accomplished yet.

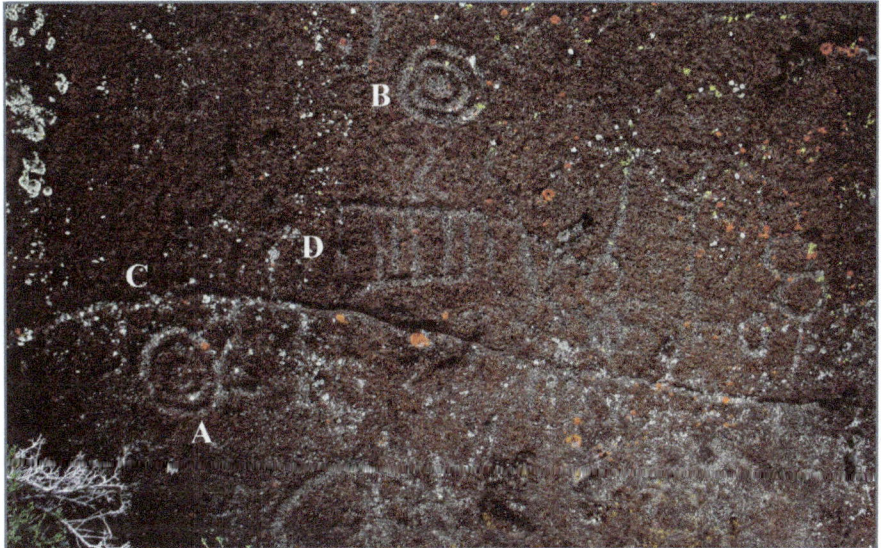

Photo 248 - Author's photo of calendar tracking panel.

Author's photo of this calendar tracking panel is on the back of the rock showing specifically the times between fall to winter, located behind the large fall season symbol, on the same keystone, designates the times specifically tracked by (D). Used for harvesting along the creek where thick wild rose bushes were cultivated and used to attract the migrating butterflies, which here the fourth generation of Monarchs are born between September and October. From here they fly south to warmer weather, and return in March/April time frame. So this site is used twice a year to catch both migrations. The natural shadow path along (C) was further highlighted by the drawer for the sun tracking. The spring symbol (A) has several shadow paths radiating from it for further clarification to the specific date of that season. The winter symbol group (B) is above the daily counter and shows connection

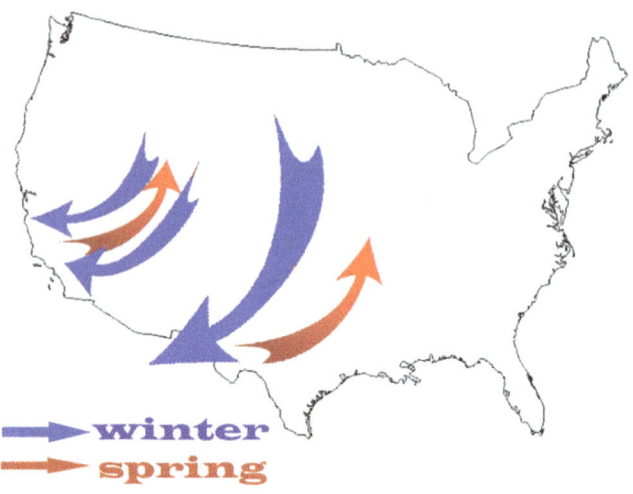

Photo 249 - Photo source: Author

paths (shadow lines) to it and the more extended counts to the right. The form of the caterpillar and the chrysalis of the count squares could be another representation of the objects as well and yet undetermined.

The Spring migration data of the same caliber is located in front and below the theme image of the butterfly head and wing image.

Author's Photo 250 of the keystone of the harvesting portion of the data, split from the migration data of the former keystone. To explain this second working panel lets see what the image represents.

Monarch butterflies go through four stages during one life cycle, and through four generations in one year. It's a little confusing but keep reading and you will understand. The four stages of the monarch butterfly life cycle are the egg, the larvae (caterpillar), the pupa (chrysalis), and the adult butterfly. The four generations are actually four different butterflies going through these four stages during one year until it is time to start over again with stage one and generation one.

ANCIENT UNIVERSAL LANGUAGE OF MAN

Photo 250 - Panel showing harvesting information for monarch chrystalis [Source: Author]

Photo 251 - Image provided by Edith Smith © showing the maturity stages of the chrysalis through the 10 days of the phase. *The Life Cycle(s) of a Monarch Butterfly*

Author's Photo 250 (A) represents the chrysalis after being harvested off the attachment location and turned upside down. Symbol (B) represents the butterfly inside it of which the actual look of the timeframe can be seen in Edith Smiths great photo 251. Symbols (C) on both sides are the ending points of the path lines of (D), whereby showing how the top of the chamber is ripped open to extract the butterfly. E shows the egg to feeding time of about two weeks when the caterpillar starts going into metamorphosis, drawn in the form of a counter for knowing when to start the countdown to harvesting th chrysalis. Symbol (F) represents the contents of the chrysalis after it is removed. From here we move to the next image to see the panel continuation to the right.

Author's Photo 252, Continuation of the harvesting along the rock right is the extended dates of the harvest. Metamorphosis times shown in symbols (H) takes about ten days, clocked with counting paths and watched very carefully. Symbol (G) is the continuation of the processing of the chrysalis and shows internal parts such as the wings.

Photo 252 - Chrysalis side information

In February and March, the final generation of hibernating monarch butterflies comes out of hibernation to find a mate. They then migrate north and east in order to find a place to lay their eggs. This starts stage one and generation one of the new year for the monarch butterfly.

In March and April the eggs are laid on milkweed plants. They hatch into baby caterpillars, also called the larvae. It takes about four days for the eggs to hatch. After about two weeks, the caterpillar will be fully-grown and start the process of metamorphosis by attaching itself to a stem or a leaf using silk and transform into a chrysalis. Within the chrysalis the old body parts of the caterpillar undergo a transformation in the next ten days, called metamorphosis, to become the the butterfly that will emerge. The monarch butterfly will emerge from the pupa and fly away, feeding on flowers in it's short life, which is only about two to six weeks. This first generation monarch will then die after laying eggs for generation two. The second generation of monarch is born in May and June, and then the third generation will be born July and August. These monarchs will go through the same four stage life cycle as the first generation, dying two to six weeks after it becomes a butterfly. The fourth generation of monarch is different and is born in September and October and goes through the same process except the butterflies do not die after two to six weeks! Instead, this generation migrates to Mexico and California and will live six to eight months until it starts the whole process over again.

Crop Growing

Photo 253 shows Lagamarsino site's main theme is growing maze, symbol seen center top.

Photo 253 - Author's photo of Lagamarsino site

Trading Vessel Demise

Here is a rock outcrop out into the lower part of the valley. This rock was a deadly obstacle to the ongoing shipping lane here and during storms sunk many ships. As seen outlined by the upside down ships and dumped cargo along the rock. A large naval armada attacked the inland lake empire here and the war recounts are given on this same outcrop.

Photo 254 - Accounts of ship demises due to losses on and around the rock outcrop near the Bishop harbor
[Source: Author]

Graveyards

Author's Photo 255, A graveyard keystone is also the theme image of a snake head. The location for a camp here in a very rough area in winter time and the village had unusual harvesting opportunity in winter. They harvested dormant rattlesnakes IN their dens.

Photo 255 - Graveyard keystone rock showing in artistic form the Theme of the camp [Source: Author]

Deer Refuge

Author's Photo 256 is of a winter site that is the feeding grounds used by deer in the Mineral County area where grass and water is plentiful.

Photo 256 - Classic keystone layout for data associated with deer winter layover zone during migrations [Source: Author]

Ancient Great Lakes Fishing

Photo 259 is Author's photo of a rock with rear side fin shaped structures that the face and lines of side gills and teeth were added to look like a type of fish or whale. Imagine the sheer size of every fish in the great lakes, some hundreds of miles long. The size and type of the species was enormous like whales.

Photo 257 - Authors photo of a whale themed panel using rock incorporation, Bishop, California.

Defensive Strongholds

Author's Photo 258 of natural rifles used as footholds to go up the rock.

This theme is a small symbol along a secret path and natural stairs going up to a secure point on the hill top that is defensible. Seen in Photo 259 is our Son standing for reference to the height of the cliff across the gap from the rock he is standing on. The small ledge leading to the riffles can be seen angled below him going up to the where the glyphs and stairs exist.

Photo 258 - Natural stairway for defensive positioning high above the valley floor in Valley Of Fire, Nevada [Source: Author]

Photo 259 - Authors photo of stairway location denoted at top of narrow natural path along rock face across from our Son as reference

Fish Harvesting

From Author's Photo 260, a collection of carvings highlighting fish heads and guts with bugs along panel.

The fish harvesting site at Walker Lake provides a great rock with panels around the base and between the many manoe grinding sites on the top from fish harvesting. Some data has been lost to vandals stealing simple symbol groups, but enough remains to show the theme of fish capturing and

Photo 260 - Photo of a fish harvesting processing rock with data on processing techniques [Source: Author]

processing. Done during spawning in April to early July! Spawn takes 6-8 week gestation plus two weeks in bed sediment. The spawning takes place up a nearby fresh water river 13,000 to 16,000 years ago. The rock bluff was just out of the water level of the lake and fish were transported from the catching pens to this harvesting location via boat to trail from the rivers wide mouth into the lake. The fish heads (A) separated from the bodies with entrails (B) attached are shown pushed over the side of the processing area (D) on top and flies and bugs (C) can be seen also symbolized feeding on the guts. The images show what should be kept and wasted.

Authors Photo 261 is of the extremely warn top from decades of fish harvesting. And some vandalism, note the rounded surface layer removed by thieves?

Further along the panel (Photo 261) to the rear of the processing rock facing the river is the symbols seen on Photo 262 of two humans (A) using a net (F) inside rock ringed (C) catch pens in the river pulling fish from them loading into a boat (D) to be sent to the rock processing center.

Photo 261 - Fish processing rock side view unaltered to clarify location of Photo 262 [Source: Author]

ANCIENT UNIVERSAL LANGUAGE OF MAN

Photo 262 - Highlighted symbols of Photo 261 showing two fisherman holding fish nets inside a rock enclosure at the river delta to the ancient lake with a boat nearby in an area located in the nearby canyon from this panel. [Source: Author]

FREMONT'S CANNON

Photo 263 is a panel with an excellent example of several key symbols in association with an American Iconic relic and event lost to time, until now. This panel is very inline to the telling of the demise of the legendary lost cannon within the confines of Western Nevada of John C. Fremont, written about in his update reports to Washington, except his own reports were contradicting. The human form (O) is surrendering (I) and "stuck" in place with no legs (K). His body is elongated (K) to show the journey, but a journey hindered the entire way. He and his head shape is tilted toward (O) the object in the discussion of his

Photo 263 - Authors highlighted photo of a petroglyph panel of the Indian witnesses rendition of Fremont's lost cannon demise and location [Source: Author]

situation which is Fremont's cannon (A), a French Mountain howitzer taken by Charles C. Fremont during his expedition through Nevada. The person shown is no other than Kit Carson, denoted by the large hat and star above the hat (N) designating "The One" as Kit was well tracked everywhere due to his ruthlessness. He was in charge of the group bringing up the canon after excorting Fremont while traveling down the canyon further toward the Sierras into what is now Walker California. In taking a more direct route due to starving animals and being far behind Fremont, ended in the cannon being flipped down a soft hill and the carriage destroyed. The symbols show many things, Kit surrendering to the cannon's demise (I), Kit waging war (H) against the canon (A) (via the contact of the war symbol between Kit and the cannon trunion) to break up the remaining portions of the carriage and it's burial along with bridals, equipment for it and 500 pounds of ammunition. You can see the war symbol of two arrowheads pointing at each other between him and the closest side of the cannon's trunnion (again H). On the other side you can see the path (F) up to the wheel broken into two segments and separated by being broken off rolling downhill (E). Behind Kit resides the very large thin war symbol (M) penetrating the other wheel the outer rim of the wheel (L). This "thin" war on it was uneventful except burial and destruction on equipment (S). The very large fully drawn in war symbol (C) is the cannons purpose in life WAR. But as you can see the symbol is broken and the arrow points do not line up completely (D), showing its ability of war is gone or reduced. The cannon symbol (A) is pointed straight down (opposite of usable canon stature) to show it is off it's normal mount and operational situation of angle. Here goes the quadruped attachment, look above it and connected (B) you will see the quadruped (P). The quadruped has the back legs (B) obviously directly attached to the rear of the canon and tilted up (P) to show stuck, buried, unable to move since no back legs exist and it is pointed vertical, opposite the correct movable and usable direction of a cannon. It has no forward legs (Q) showing no forward movement being possible. The horns (R) are flat, straight, thick and inline with the head symbol and up bent "broken" at the back to show the dramatic ending. It has a rounded underbelly (Q) in incorporation with an arched up back (P) to match and even curves into a tail, all depicting a full buried ending. Though more of the decipherment of the body is needed, generally all of the weight and amounts of the cannon's gear is broken (back) and dumped together into a pit (filled in pit being the outlined shape of the quadruped in general). Observe the very thin lines (J) used to connect many items on the panel to assist the user as I discussed before. This panel shows them great, because the general area was so close the Indians shadowing the group did not dare be discovered as they would be killed knowing such location and thus only scratched this panel completely with no hammering to make sounds at all. There were two, maybe three observers taking note, but only two "peeking" eyes above the rock are drawn at the top of the boulder, a writer may be a third. Other data is included around the remaining panel and many lines are to light to survive time in great shape, but the canyon path and hills it traveled are listed, group size and more on when it met its demise.

Documented official history outlines Fremont's exploration was to find a path for wagons to travel west and find passageways and a legendary river that flowed to the Pacific. The thought was that a cannon has a wheelbase like a wagon so transporting it through proves a wagon could also travel the same route? I believe the cannons were brought and Fremont's very large group sent, to find the lost city of gold and Aztec treasure. A canon and arms against Indians is kind of overkill then, just firing it cleared entire valleys of active Indian camps.

As I have been around Government USGS Geologists growing up I learned "official" reports of work turned in are always fudged to show work is being completed every day, but in reality work is done in large groups of time, then the smaller tasks performed are covered up with fudging in those days stringing out that field work. The same is true for Fremont and discussing the fact the canon and group took a different more direct route and him not present within the distances he was from the canon would be very bad, thus it was covered up some on where exactly everything and everyone was during that event. This would be similar to losing a stealth jet in enemy territory today.

> An excerpt of Fremont's report follows of the cannon;
> "Frémont's Report to Washington January 25-29, 1844
> Frémont: Feb 28th
> ".....To-night we did not succeed in getting the Howitzer into camp.
> ..... Frémont: January 29th.
> :...One of these places we expected to reach to-night; and some time
> being required to bring up the gun....The principal stream still running
> through an impractical cañon, we ascended a very steep hill, which proved
> afterwards the last and fatal obstacle to our little howitzer, which was
> finally abandoned at this place......They had not succeeded
> in getting the howitzer beyond the place mentioned, and
> where it had been left by Mr. Preuss in obedience
> to my orders..."

Photo 264 - Author's photo of the sister cannon to Fremont's S/N #3 on display at Carson City, Nevada. State Museum

Photo 265 - Author's photo of the front of #3 cannon at Carson City, Nv. State Museum

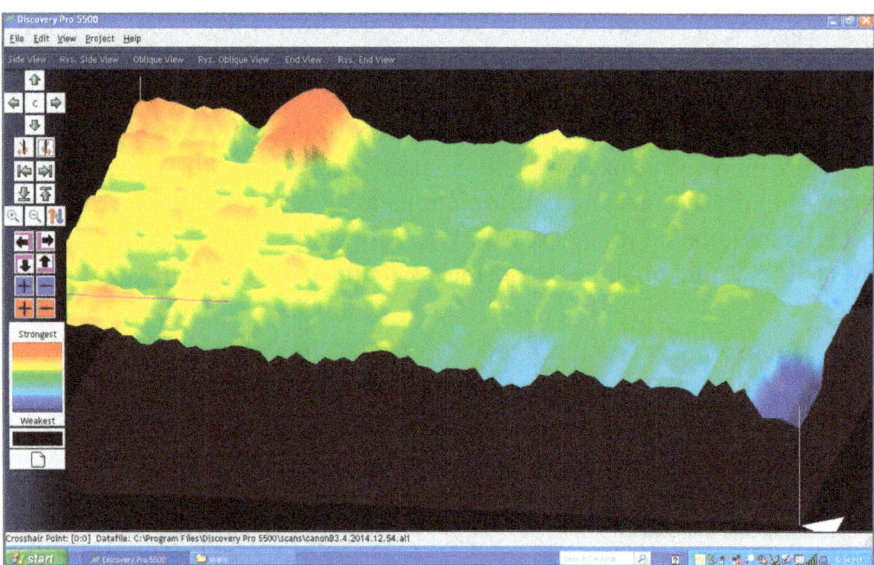

Photo 266 - Author's scan, running gauss detection across the valley which defined two target pits seven feet to nine feet deep.

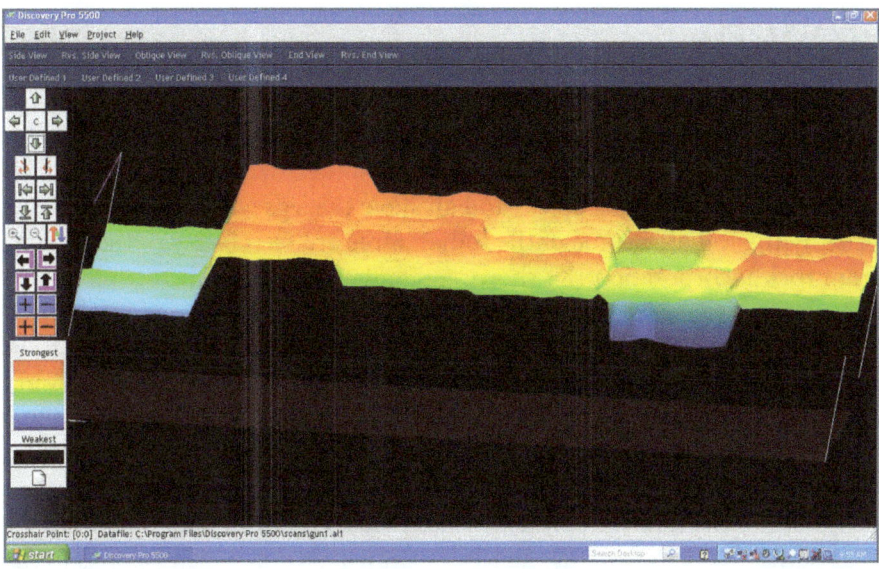

Photo 267 - Authors scan of cannon in a more defined space showing the target in blue.

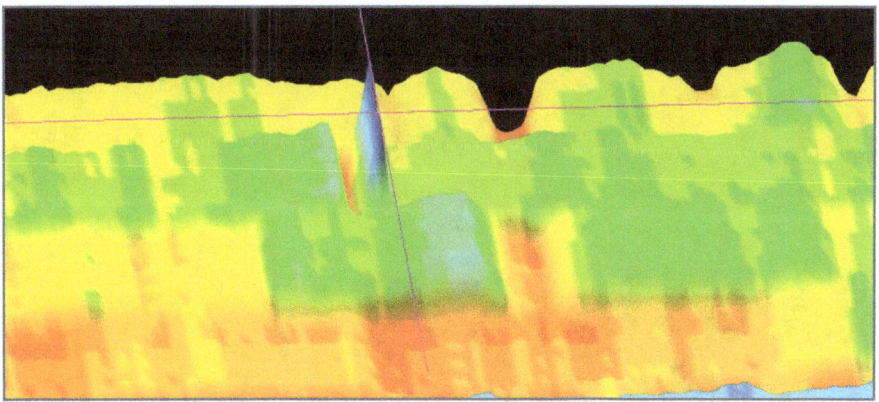

Photo 268 - A reverse image to better show the buried target and adjoining pits of equipment and munitions.

SPANISH

Photo 269 is a key rock designating the surrender of thirteen Spanish including a commander, seen here carrying the kings crown guide on (B) and has the large hat (A), (representing his real hat and that he is in charge) and wearing a cape (H). Represented are 11 workers with smaller hats (D) all surrendering with hands up (F) and all show the legs wide in a jump of surprise by the Indians. Some of the Indian force are seen below in the shadow from rock incorporation (K) showing circular capture of the Spanish force (G) coming from the raid starting at night. Everyone died and was buried in mass graves. There is more around the rock explaining the campaign including a great representation of the excavated mine being shown several times the Spanish worked in. One is rock incorporation visible in the top just right of center where a natural hole is outlined and drawn from (indicating mine). Their treasure was buried as well, but unfound. The group appears to be the area's Captain who picked up the precious metals from the mines for the Spanish King (known as the Kings' Crown, or that which belongs to the king through taxing of the metals mining). Seen to the lower right the camp that was here was wiped out on the start of the raid by sweeping fire (E) and several died in the initial fire and combat. Others survived the initial fire and then the full on attack before being killed.

Photo 269 - Spanish surrender panel [Source: Author]

This single rough panel seen in Photo 270, I photographed and highlighted, is located beside the main panel on a separate rock. Showing the remaining survivors as they continued to bury their dead in the face of their own death. Crosses were hastily erected from axe cut tree branches and wrapped together with leather. You can see the man on right with a shovel has the "brave" dog tail behind him showing courage. The cross between depicts the burial crosses made which were a row of 3 smaller crosses depicting a mass grave and one large cross set upon the hilltop depicting the gravesite proper. Seen to the left is a helper, both being killed after the feat and probably buried in the same hole they dug. All that is left is the square rock formations of the camp and the fallen crosses beside this petroglyph.

Photo 270 - Authors photo of a brave individual spanish laborer burying his fellow dead knowing he will die after this task [Source: Author]

ALIEN VISITORS

Drawn in Photo 271 are several locating star groups (A) and the path of the moon from a full moon (B) (with bat inside it) through several days cycle until no moon. This amount of directional star information shows a location rather than a needed date and time. The lower right side of the rock under the overhang to show shadow/dark rather than in the ground has a unique shadow symbol (C) attached to it. A great symbol to show evidence a lightly pecked symbol is not a type or style but usable way to draw to represent and just like a shadow has less substance. It is drawn longer and lighter and attached correctly at the appendages to display "shadow at night." From the direction of light to cast the shadow you see the circle "object" (D) with the trail of fire (E) behind it and the object is in a downward heading position (North). A comet three tail symbol is drawn with specific tail directions for the actual tail angles and thus different than the fire symbol. You can see downward path lines (F) together showing trails of light coming down on the object from above like meteors but without fire, just trails or the paths of landing. Behind and obvious is the star system location the object came from.

Photo 271 - Authors photo of alien contact [Source: Author]

To the objects left there is a larger human symbol (G) with downward bent arms holding something (H) in the closest hand and a calendar (I) above him to the far left above.

The most interesting combination is the man (J) under the full moon showing the clear beckoning outreached arm (K) toward the figures (N) under the "object" and his backhand (L) extended and pointing down "here" inviting others to him. The path (M) of his hand shows the connection that the invitation was accepted. The most interesting thing is his very pronounced outward straight tail (O) out his back showing much "courage" in doing his act. Close up of the little "far" persons (again N) are 5 unusual made shapes he invites. The path of the shadow human shows his shadow is clearly seen at night due to the bright light of the object and his hand (P) controls a path (Q) toward and between two circles.

The valley even today displays very unusual weather patterns and I have been two feet from multiple lightning strikes simultaneously trying to escape in a truck from a downpour, been sunburned walking out due to flat tires from the valley on a sunny noon and returned with two feet of snow on the ground two hours later. And been in sunny skies and before getting back to the truck was in a painful hail storm. We broke down once there miles from town midsummer and we encountered unusual grinding and scratching noises at dusk that echoed and then had a 6.0+ earthquake right under our feet an hour later. I remain away from the area anytime any clouds are visible now and the lightning storms in it can be seen for miles.

The Ancient Floating City of the Pyramid

Photo 272 is at Pyramid Lake, Nevada, that the history of the Si-Te-Cah read-headed giants lived on the last remaining floating city in the west.

Photo 272 - Author's photo of a large panel group beside Pyramid Lake, Nevada, shows the major theme of fish scales.

Photo 273 - Author's photo, Also along Pyramid Lake exists this spectacular rock incorporation to show a fish with open mouth and the eye.

Trains

Photos 274-276 by Ernie Winters "On the backroads" collection, Fremont Indian state park panel showing train petroglyphs.

Photo 274

Photo 275

Photo 276

ANCIENT UNIVERSAL LANGUAGE OF MAN

Photo 277 - Author's photo, Walker Lake a Indian onlooker scratched this light petroglyph near the railroad tracks of a caboose.

Photo 278 - Author's photo, Note the caboose style, some having the rounded window ports for viewing forward. Note also the smokestack, rear steps, lanterns and top light box all seen in the above panel using various symbols as designators, key to getting insight into the Universal Language decipherment.

Lake Fowl Hunting

On the ancient shores of Lake Lahontan are hundreds of bird hunting sites including this one in Photo 279. The best sites to hunt are coves where birds can take refuge from winds and larger wakes. Larger rock piles offer superb hiding locations or this giant rock near the water edge. It has been argued the right (west) side pictographs are original because they "appear to be authentic, both stylistically and in their execution" (Tuohy 1983) Great Basin Rock Art, page 13, and that is why it was probably not done by Curtis's Indian subject photographed painting it. On the contrary, the less faded and UNstylistic and UNrealistic symbols, groups and configurations of that panel is completely made up by an Indian who does not know the language! For one the photographic images show contact with a brush equal in thickness to the symbols toward the lower portion. There is no real thickness variation needed to complete the path lines properly, they are all one thickness relating to so many opposite meanings it is clear they mean nothing. They are just another legal defacement of historic petroglyphs. In contrast the upper part of the panel on the bottom of the overhang is of importance and was original. The possibility of real images being under some of the graffiti accepted below could be a reality but we can't be sure now.

Photo 279 - Author's photo showing actual North facing pictograph aging.

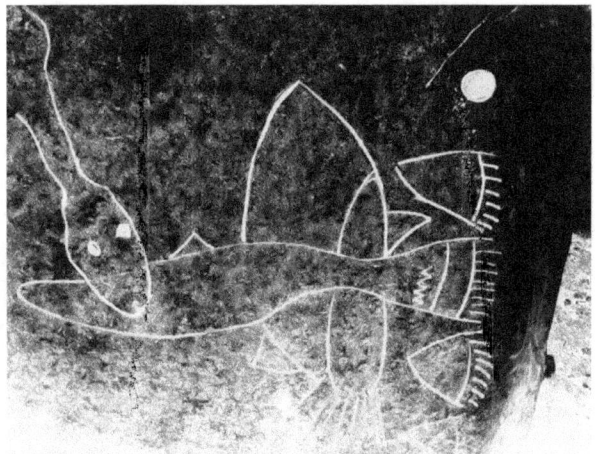

Photo 280 - Drawing overlay of pictograph courtesy of Carl Bjork. A look initially it can be imagined a head eating a fish but a closer inspection reveals you see the goose and duck web feet apparently separated from the tail bobbing of ducks and geese hunted from this cove rock.

Obsidian Mining

Many sites all inhabitants of the globe used widely was the many mining quarry's for rock, minerals, and metals. I found a great site (Photo 281) with multiple colored obsidian stretching down a canyon for a mile. The canyon was hidden and after a lifetime of hunting the region I finally ran across it by accident. The panels were in deep snow and some information missing until I get back to it. Beyond the pits under the rock faces there is no longer digging evidence except the millions of manmade chips down the slope seeming to go forever (Photo 282). The fact this is the only obsidian near a great hunting location is a plus and a surprise as I track obsidian deposits and prior the closest I thought to this site was over six miles away at the bottom of the mountain range.

Photo 281 - Author's photo of one panel designating the locations of the mines down the long canyon.

Photo 282 - Author's photo of the ground littered with obsidian dug and chips left from sizing down transportable sized chunks.

Acknowledgments

As I pursued this lifelong fascination with shear tenacity, I met many along the way with the same spirit, all asking "it must mean something!" I come away after this book knowing I am just another step toward my goal and not at the end of my journey like I thought I might be. In closing one chapter I inadvertently exposed more, but this time I know they are all attainable. For when you shed the chains of doubt you realize it is you alone on a path you were destined to follow, and more so to accomplish!

I could not have conceived of making a book a decade ago, my youth spent wondering in life's many directions never believing I would ever clamp down so hard to make such a work of passion. I owe so much to so many I am at a loss to attempt describing the external influences that led me to this point. Above all to thank is God, allowing me a life of curiosity and unique insight. Of the stars who have shined in my life, the brightest has been my loving wife Dede! To her I owe so much and lean on her for all things, we were soul mates since before time itself. My fascination of the lands goes to two fascinating people themselves, my Grandfather Richard Jack (Dick) Hegg and my dear friend Vic Despres. Who both took me out there into the vast desert I once thought barren, but found it was full of wonder and amazement. My mentor and my teacher who taught me artistic expression, and mother by choice Willow J. Phillips. My love for rocks goes to my great friend E. B. (Bart) Ekren, retired U.S.G.S. Geologist and WW II veteran who served as a machine gunner in the Battle of the Bulge. Thank you for your patience, insight and training in the lifetime of geologic quests we have been on. And to my loving sister, April Sawtelle, who has been my anchor, always helping and guiding me and keeping me steadfast on this journey. And to the adversary in my life, I have encountered you enough to realize you are my springboard to success!

Index

Symbols

1D 23, 145
2D 23, 66, 98, 144, 197
3D 23, 98, 99, 144, 145
12 month yearly calendar 76

A

acid test 13, 14
Adams, Ken 186
afterlife 84
air 61, 64, 71
alien 231
analemma 133, 134, 136, 137, 138, 139, 146, 147
ancient 4, 131, 134, 147, 157, 173, 189, 194, 199, 208
ancient empire 4, 5, 6, 66, 84, 94, 157, 160, 176, 177, 178, 181, 190, 200, 211
ancient great lakes 6, 21, 49, 51, 61, 65, 66, 84, 87, 90, 121, 157, 160, 175, 176, 177, 178, 180, 182, 183, 184, 185, 187, 188, 189, 190, 191, 198, 200, 206, 210, 221, 224, 236
ancients 4, 5, 69, 77, 83, 114, 158, 159, 176, 180, 190, 200, 206
animal 13, 20, 47, 54, 61, 62, 69, 70, 73, 88, 106, 123, 148, 149, 164, 189, 201
animal trail 60, 126, 188
animation 22, 123
Arapaho 17

arborglyphs 39, 45
arc 95, 96, 97
archeoastronomy 85, 114
Arizona 72, 100
arrow 16, 19
arrowheads 19
arrow point 17
artistic representation 40
ash 71, 161
astrological 87
Autumn 48, 94, 96, 97, 107, 114, 132, 135, 138, 207, 213, 215
Aztec 5, 6, 227

B

Babel 2
ballast 85
bar 207
baskets 145
bat 161, 231
beginning 53, 132
Bible 5
bird 24, 57, 68, 161, 201
Bishop, California 178, 191, 210
bison 70
blankets 98
blinds 13, 44
blocking 49, 167
boat 64, 66, 85, 87, 164, 178, 180, 189, 191, 193, 224
  docks 190

body 15, 22, 23, 24, 27, 28, 30, 31, 32, 49, 50, 56, 57, 59, 63, 64, 65, 66, 128, 142, 155, 166, 168, 172, 173, 195, 206, 225, 232
   arm movement 22
   dexterity 22
   feet types 63, 155
   finger 16, 24, 27, 28, 30, 32, 33, 34, 53, 95, 104, 142, 144, 145, 167, 172, 173, 195, 196, 197
   fingertip 32, 53
   foot 150, 162, 172, 173
   form 71
   gestures 31
   motion 14, 15
   mouth 20
   movement 15, 30, 36
   movements 23
   position 17
   thumb 53, 95, 104, 195
bones 108
boulder 54, 87, 227
bracketing 47, 77, 91, 112, 123, 126, 207
brain 18, 30, 31, 32, 63
butterflies 214, 215, 216, 217, 219

C

calendar 94, 215
California 178, 191, 210
camel 74, 165
camp 53, 60, 128, 156, 178, 188, 230, 231
cannon 226
canyon 13, 54
captured 51, 53
cargo 64, 191
Carl Bjork 21
cart 61
Cassiopeia 77, 91, 92, 93, 94, 106, 107, 134
cave 6, 23, 39, 44, 45, 49, 50, 60, 149, 159, 188, 194, 195, 196, 197, 199, 200, 206
celestial movements 61, 72, 75
center dot 107
Chinese 17, 26

circles 17, 34, 35, 41, 53, 54, 55, 65, 67, 75, 80, 81, 83, 88, 94, 95, 97, 100, 104, 114, 119, 120, 138, 145, 168, 195, 196, 230
circumference data 78, 102, 137, 143
cities 5, 176
classrooms 4
clay disks 45
cliff 20, 48, 54, 58, 106, 107, 109, 162, 197
clocked positions 91
clockwise 136
Clovis People 194
combination drawings 22, 40, 61, 114, 120, 138
combined symbols 36, 107, 114
complex 27, 52, 53, 106, 131
complex symbols 24, 35
compressing 104
concentric circles 36
confusion 25
connectors 43
continuous paths 131
Contract 105
core 27, 51, 52, 53, 131
   combinations 95
   meaning 13, 62
   path 37, 53, 61
   point 61
core meaning 132
core symbol 14, 24, 35, 36, 37, 46, 53, 55, 75, 96
   path 34
Coso Range 65, 178
count 78, 80, 81, 100, 130
counterclockwise 136, 138
counting paths 218
count lines 129
count squares 216
courage 232
Court of Antiquity 78, 185
covered 63
covering 59
cracks 39, 70, 87, 88, 119, 152
creator 43, 64, 88, 91, 145, 148, 150
creek 128, 130, 215

cremation 159
crop growing 219
crops 40, 46, 47, 66, 102, 125, 178, 188
  cycles 94, 107
  harvest 128, 173, 217, 220
crosses 48, 138
cryptology 11
cupulas 44, 45
curved 51, 61
curving path 51
cycle 35, 37, 71, 76, 85, 132, 191, 231

D

dashed lines 46
data 44, 48, 61, 62, 87, 106, 216
dead 84, 85, 132, 156, 157, 159
death 4, 63, 71, 84, 85, 128, 153, 154, 211
Death Valley 181
deception 12
decipher 12, 13, 14, 24, 27, 34, 41, 54, 68, 70, 76, 87, 135, 148, 165, 178, 200, 205, 211
deer 47, 64, 108, 221
defensive 162, 189, 222
deforested 5
descending 37
Desert Research Institute 185, 186
direction 68, 104
distance 64
division lines 81
docks 65, 66, 85, 176, 177, 178, 191, 193
dog tails 20, 24, 25, 163, 231
dot 32, 34, 100, 114
dotted lines 46
double spiral 136
drawer 40, 48, 59
drilled 78
drugs 4, 19, 83

E

earth mounds 45
earthquake 49, 210, 232
East 112
Easter Island 5

eclipse 167, 168
edge 107
Egyptian 5, 6, 17, 26
elephants 189, 212
elevation 63, 64
elliptical 134, 135
empty 31
ending 34, 53, 68, 132
enemies 87
environment 13, 14, 24, 68
equinox 96, 100, 135
expanding 81, 104, 105
extra data 78
eyes 30, 32, 42, 160, 167

F

family 4, 124, 158, 159
fear 69
fences 54
fire 56, 71, 161, 162, 188, 191, 230
first 32, 53, 81, 95, 138
fish harvesting 223, 224
fishing 47
fixed combinations 36
fixed set symbol group 132
fixed spot 96
flee 71
flight 68
floating cities 6, 84, 175, 176, 188, 233
flood 49, 52, 71
flowing 51
fog 23, 48
food 5, 47, 66, 112, 177
forward 65
Fremont, Charles C. 6, 189, 225, 226
frozen pond 51, 52
future 5, 168

G

generic symbol 40
geoglyphs 39, 42, 45, 55, 188, 189
Germany 12
giants 4, 6, 7, 10, 11, 181, 207, 233
Gilgal 116
glacier 177

global warming 5
goods 71, 177, 182
grasp 53
graveyard 48, 57, 85, 124, 127, 128, 153, 154, 155, 156, 157, 158, 159, 160, 188, 212, 220
  burial 6, 125, 159, 164
  central 87, 157, 159
  flower 153, 154
  graves 128, 154, 230
  ritual precessions 116
  satellite graveyards 158
  site 86
Greeks 5
Grimes Point, Fallon, Nevada 21, 164, 177
group 24, 27, 61, 70, 71, 75, 114, 124, 153, 167

H

harbor 65, 176, 188, 191, 192
harvesting 44, 130, 154, 215, 216, 218
Hav-musuvs 182
Hawthorne 87, 185, 206, 210
head 22, 23, 30, 31, 63, 66, 123, 128, 225
hearing 18
heavens 116
held 53
herd 73, 164
Hickison Summit 122
hidden caves 60, 149, 150, 194, 197, 198, 200, 201, 202
hiding 11
hill 59
holes 78
holy sites 48, 154
horns 62, 63, 64, 67
horse 64, 70, 164
hot 63
hours 96
human 22, 23, 24, 25, 33, 47, 49, 54, 61, 62, 63, 64, 66, 67, 69, 71, 72, 74, 107, 131, 138, 142, 149, 153, 155, 164, 172, 190, 200, 207, 215, 224, 225, 232
human form 70, 71, 150

hunting 13, 44, 47, 54, 60, 66, 87, 89, 93, 106, 124, 177, 188, 189, 236

I

ice age 6, 37, 177
ice symbol group 6, 51, 52, 66
ideogram 4
idiographs 61
Inca 5
Indians 4, 11, 15, 16, 22, 26, 27, 43, 54, 63, 161, 162, 181, 194, 226, 227, 230, 236
initial drawing 44
intaglios 45

J

journey 62, 63, 64, 66, 71, 73, 84, 85, 149, 225

K

keystone 40, 41, 47, 59, 91, 92, 116, 123, 128, 215, 220, 230, 231
killing 62
Kit Carson 226
Knowth 146

L

Lagamarsino 125, 185, 219
land 61, 64, 66, 73, 85, 124, 129, 165, 178, 180
land ownership 126, 130
land travel 71
language 14, 15, 23
layers 47, 49
layout 38
legs 63, 64, 65, 225, 226, 230
Lewis, Meriwether 4
lightning 47
line 32, 41, 43, 46, 48, 75, 107, 123, 130, 145, 147, 226, 227
linear 17, 23, 145
lizards 200, 201, 202
looping path 53
Lucifer's trident 56

M

magic dancing 74
magnetic poles 5
main story 40, 47
major and minor standstill 83
mammoth 164
man 24, 123, 180, 206, 232
map 54, 178, 186, 189, 191
marker 195
Mark Twain 162
mastodons 165
Mayan 5, 26
measurement stone 79
Medicine Wheel 45
megalithic 5, 39, 114, 146
message 22, 41
micro decipherment 148, 200
migration 63, 64, 73, 106, 158, 188, 214
mine 161, 162, 177, 194, 230, 237
Mineral County 206
Moai 5
modern symbols 5, 6, 16
modern thinking 74
modifications 40
month 75, 76, 77, 100, 104, 111, 120, 131, 132, 134, 137, 138, 146, 147, 166
    April 136, 137, 138, 139, 147, 215, 218, 224
    August 136, 137, 138, 139, 219
    calendar 134
    count 77
    cycle 93, 147
    December 136, 137
    February 136, 138, 218
    January 136, 137, 138, 142
    July 136, 139, 219, 224
    June 136, 139, 142, 219
    March 136, 215, 218
    May 136, 137, 219
    November 136
    October 136, 215, 219
    September 136, 137, 138, 139, 215, 219
monument 5, 6

moon 42, 53, 68, 72, 75, 77, 78, 79, 80, 81, 83, 92, 94, 102, 135, 143, 162, 168, 172, 173, 207, 231
    count symbol 100
    cycle 78
    full moon 77, 208, 232
    lunar counting 168
    lunar cycles 75, 131, 132
    lunar eclipse 173
    lunar month 80
    lunar standstills 77
    moonrise 83
    phase counting 72
    tracking 78
    waxing phase 81
motion 15, 123, 167
mound 59, 146
mountain 20, 86, 87, 149, 150, 151, 152, 157, 160, 188
mountain range 49, 70
movement 15, 32, 33, 49, 61, 62, 64, 67, 102, 134, 135
Myans 6

N

Nasca Lines 45, 147
natural 15, 30, 42, 54, 67, 69, 72, 77, 123, 132, 134, 152, 154, 162, 167, 177, 197, 200
    crack 102
    form 68
    hole 39
    path 134
    shadow shapes 121
neck 63, 64, 66
negation 26
neutral location 62, 70, 88
Nevada 6, 40, 45, 60, 67, 78, 90, 122, 159, 184, 185, 188, 189, 193, 201, 206, 210, 226, 233
Nevada Backroads 99
New Grange 45
new year 146
night 68, 75, 77, 80, 92, 94, 96, 130, 188, 208, 231

North 20
North America 84, 85, 92, 163, 177
nothing 30, 31
numbers 75

O

object 32, 33, 54, 107, 216, 225
obliterating 43
occupation 47, 122, 123, 124, 178
on top 59
Orion Pillars 84, 85, 86, 191
Orion's Belt 87
outline 44
out of round 109
oval 135, 136, 137, 139
ownership 125, 128
oxidation 38

P

pack animals 71, 162, 163, 164, 165
packs 64
paint 45, 100, 166, 167
Paiute 6, 9, 181
panel 13, 24, 25, 36, 40, 43, 44, 47, 49, 51, 54, 60, 64, 66, 67, 68, 70, 71, 78, 87, 88, 102, 109, 112, 120, 142, 144, 148, 149, 208, 216, 226, 227
patenation 38
path 13, 20, 21, 24, 27, 28, 29, 32, 33, 35, 36, 46, 47, 49, 51, 53, 55, 59, 60, 64, 67, 71, 77, 88, 95, 104, 107, 111, 121, 133, 138, 148, 150, 154, 156, 161, 178, 180, 189, 207, 226
  continuous 215
  line 48, 90, 100, 137
  meaning 48
  open 65
  symbol 63
path line 231
peace 2, 7, 19
pear cactus harvesting 173
pecking 46
pecks 150

petroglyph 5, 6, 7, 8, 9, 12, 13, 15, 19, 38, 39, 45, 47, 65, 70, 87, 95, 99, 158, 164, 176, 177, 183, 187, 231
  decipherment 198
  location 175
  panel 13
  sites 178
  styles 3
Phaistos Disk 147
physical location 53
physical object 32
pictograph 20, 39, 45, 54
pinching 53
pinyon pine nuts 125
pinyon pines 126
pit 87, 159
Planet X 5
plot 124, 125
point 16, 24, 32, 33, 34, 35, 36, 44, 46, 53, 61, 95, 96
pointer 120, 194
polar stars 90
Polynesians 5, 6
Pompeii 6
pottery 45, 98, 145
precession 85, 135
processing 62
procession 84
progression 95, 110, 121
projection 68
pull 105
push 105
pyramid 45, 132, 194, 233
Pyramid Lake 7, 233

Q

quadruped 61, 62, 63, 64, 65, 66, 67, 70, 72, 74, 81, 123, 144, 149, 150, 165, 201, 226
quarters 135

R

radial lines 81
radiating lines 104, 120, 121, 123
radius 107

rain 47, 48, 51, 71, 102, 104
rattlesnake harvesting 40
reader 41, 48
red 20, 70
red hair giants 4, 6
red ochre 55
Red Rock Pass 186
retreat 69
reverse 135
ridge 125
ring 80, 107, 114, 121
rings 83
rising 37
river 49
rock 24, 37, 38, 40, 42, 59, 67, 70, 74, 78, 88, 89, 107, 114, 128, 137, 145, 149, 150, 152, 159, 162
rock incorporation 38, 40, 47, 59, 60, 102, 119, 126, 149, 163, 197, 207, 213, 215, 230
rock surface 38
rock texture 48, 151
Romans 5
rotation 92, 93
route 128, 180
rugs 145

S

sacred site 155
sacrifice 6
sands 13
sap 188
satellite 158
scared 57
scratch 15, 43, 46, 87, 107, 226, 232
season 92, 94, 95, 100, 102, 106, 107, 109, 120, 123, 130, 143, 166
    symbol 94, 97, 98, 102, 109, 111, 112, 114, 119, 121, 126, 127, 130, 131, 134, 146, 208, 213
season symbol group 27, 63, 98, 137 134
serpent 132
Serpent Mound 146

shadow 40, 43, 47, 67, 68, 77, 78, 91, 98, 107, 110, 118, 119, 120, 121, 122, 123, 129, 130, 132, 134, 135, 140, 144, 148, 215, 230, 232
    casting 78, 111, 121, 139
    incorporation 40, 109, 114
    line 119
    movement 134
    path 68, 78, 104, 120, 123, 135, 137, 138, 215
    reversal 134
    spiral 147
    stick 134, 135
    tracking 75
sheep 64
shield 78, 80
ship 65, 84, 124, 177, 181, 188, 190, 191, 192, 220
Shoshone 54
sign 22, 23
Signal Hill 100
sign language 15, 17, 19, 22, 23, 27, 28, 31, 32, 36, 59, 95, 104, 105, 132, 144, 172, 195
Sign Language Among North American Indians Compared With That Among Other Peoples and Deaf-Mutes First Annual Report of the Bureau of Ethnology to the 1881 (Garrick Mallery) 15, 17, 18
site 4, 15, 25, 41, 48, 85, 114, 132, 155, 178
Si-Te-Cah 6, 11, 207, 233
site location 187
sketches 43
sky 39, 42, 47, 48, 70, 73, 85, 95, 96, 133, 134, 135, 140
small people 4
smoke 23
snake 40, 127, 128, 206, 207
snow 38, 47, 48, 49, 121, 237
solar 38, 41, 42, 130, 167, 172
    crossover 102, 133, 135, 136, 138, 139, 147
    daily counter 215

daily cycle 81
daily tracking 75, 117
day 96, 100, 111, 112, 130, 132, 148
daylight 91, 95
daytime 92
day tracking 75
eclipse 172, 173
flares 5
solstice 77, 95, 100
symbols 166
tracking 130
Solstice
  95, 129, 133, 135
sound 30
South Africa 147
Spanish 56, 162, 230
Spanish miner 56, 161
Spartan 12
spiral 25, 36, 131, 132, 134, 135, 136,
  137, 138, 140, 142, 144, 146
Spirit Man 159
Spring
  13, 20, 48, 49, 51, 54, 88, 94, 95, 96,
    97, 114, 121, 126, 132, 135, 138,
    148, 149, 177, 206, 210, 213, 216
springs 89, 178, 188
square 71, 124, 130, 144
staff length 78
standstills 77, 94, 102
star 24, 33, 42, 77, 84, 86, 87, 92, 226,
  231
starting point 34, 53, 68
Stonehenge 45, 114, 115
storm 7, 49, 71, 205
story 13, 25, 27, 38, 39, 40, 41, 58, 66,
  67, 68, 70, 71, 112, 123, 126, 152, 162,
  207, 215
  setup 38, 39
  storyboard 40
  telling 22
styles 15, 44, 48, 50, 145
Sumerians 5
Summer 48, 80, 94, 96, 97, 98, 114, 133,
  135, 138, 139, 142, 213, 215

sun 43, 68, 71, 78, 79, 92, 94, 95, 96, 98,
  102, 110, 112, 122, 130, 132, 133, 134,
  135, 138, 140, 148, 167, 172, 214
  crossovers 94
  day symbol 121
  marker 111
  path 120, 129, 134, 146
  position tracking 47
  shadow 121
  Solstices 83
  sunrise 37
  sunset 37
  symbol 47, 111
  tracking 94, 121, 129, 136, 215
supplies 65, 66, 149, 162, 164, 165, 178,
  200
surface 40
surrender 6, 225, 230
survival 30, 34, 41, 47, 94, 178, 194
symbol 2, 10, 11, 12, 13, 14, 15, 19, 22,
  23, 25, 27, 34, 35, 38, 46, 54, 57, 63,
  66, 70, 85, 86, 98, 110, 131, 156, 168,
  196
  combination 40, 43, 47, 48, 49, 138,
    207
  counting 80
  group 13, 34, 51, 61, 62, 63, 66, 70, 81,
    95, 148

T

tablets 98
tail 25, 63, 64, 88, 138, 139, 232
tarantula 206, 207
task 24, 116
tattooing 39, 123, 152, 215
tee pee rings 44
temperatures 23
theme 40, 53, 68, 205, 213, 219, 222
thunder 47
time 5, 36, 40, 63, 66, 68, 71, 87, 90,
  104, 107, 109, 110, 114, 121, 122, 123,
  131, 147
toes 71, 173
top 55
topic 25, 33, 36, 38, 43

tortured 6
Tower of Babel 5
track 77, 83, 107, 109, 122
  line 78, 130
  shadows 122
trade 6, 47, 74, 177, 178, 188, 189, 208, 211, 220
  goods 65, 165, 178, 188
  routes 178, 187
  supplies 65
trail 60, 149, 188
train 63, 234
transport 65, 98, 158
travel 47, 53, 63, 64, 65, 66, 67, 68, 69, 70, 74, 123, 167
tree 5, 13, 54, 231
Troy 147
Truckee River 78
tufa 7, 8

U

UFO 182
United States 183
Universal Language 2, 5, 6, 12, 13, 14, 15, 20, 22, 23, 28, 35, 36, 37, 41, 43, 45, 47, 48, 49, 51, 52, 60, 61, 62, 63, 66, 67, 69, 70, 74, 76, 92, 112, 114, 123, 131, 153, 156, 166, 172, 173, 195, 200, 201, 205, 215

V

Valley of Fire 45, 123
vandalism 83, 84, 85
Verneukpan 147
vertical 20, 51
viewer 23, 31
visual stimuli 18
volcanic eruption 47, 71, 87
vulva form 54, 111

W

wagons 163
Walker Lake 11, 175, 185, 193, 223
war 4, 6, 7, 11, 12, 16, 19, 21, 40, 47, 67, 70, 78, 158, 164, 188, 189, 191, 206, 207, 208, 220, 226
warning 5, 57, 155
water 6, 7, 10, 13, 49, 51, 52, 60, 66, 73, 85, 86, 88, 89, 90, 112, 121, 148, 156, 162, 165, 177, 178, 180, 182, 186, 210
water waves 49
waveform 49
weather 23, 40, 47, 48, 49, 73, 92, 112, 131, 177, 191
week 75, 77, 133
West 4, 112
White Mountain City 162
white people 4
white sign 15
wind 47, 51
Winter 48, 68, 94, 95, 96, 97, 98, 106, 107, 126, 128, 142, 215, 220
  Season Symbol Pack 149
wood 89, 162, 193
world 138, 177
writer 13, 25, 38, 39, 40, 41, 43, 46, 66, 69, 70
written languages 10, 17, 33, 84

Y

year 40, 43, 47, 68, 75, 76, 77, 90, 92, 94, 95, 96, 107, 110, 111, 122, 131, 134, 135, 138, 142, 147, 158, 177

Z

zigzag 48, 49, 59, 121, 142, 162

www.ingramcontent.com/pod-product-compliance
Lightning Source LLC
Chambersburg PA
CBHW082037230426
43670CB00016B/2688